BETWEEN THE CATTAILS & THE BULRUSHES

AN AUTOBIOGRAPHY

Gordon F. Ekberg

Between the Cattails and the Bulrushes
An Autobiography

By Gordon F. Ekberg
© Gay Ekberg 2017
ISBN: 978-0-9981476-2-8

First Edition

Cover design by Evangeline (Ekberg) Johnson

Format by Minion Editing & Design www.joyminion.com

Printed in the United States of America

Order from:

Victor Lundeen Company
126 West Lincoln Avenue
Fergus Falls, MN 56537
218.736.5433 or 800.346.4870

Grant County Historical Society and Museum
115 2nd Avenue NE
Elbow Lake, MN 56531
218.685.4864

Lawndale Farm Wildlife Art Gallery
15197 240th Avenue
Herman, MN 56248
320.677.2687 or 320.815.9190
lawndale@frontiernet.net

Dedication

Dedicated to my wife, Gay,
and our children Kris Ann, Amy, Joel, Vangie and John

Acknowledgments

We, the family of Gordon Ekberg, thank the following people for their encouragement, guidance and ongoing inspiration to Gordon in the writing this book:

Carole Butcher (Wordsmith);

Margie Andersen (neighbor who encouraged Gordon's writing);

Family, Friends and Neighbors (who preordered books);

Betsy Ostenson (Lake Region Arts Council liason);

Joy Minion (editor); and

**The Lake Region Arts Council
for awarding the Legacy Arts and Cultural Heritage Grant
to Gordon for the editing and printing of this book.**

Preface

*B*etween the Cattails and the Bulrushes tells the journey of a shy, well-mannered boy in the 1930s, raised as an only child on his beloved Lawndale Farm. From a challenging birth to challenges on the country school playground to close-call experiences, Gordon persevered through sheer determination and a gusto for life. His lifelong compassion and kindness to all—friend and foe, animals and the environment—led to many leadership roles in church, organizations and community at levels up to international in scope. He was transformed by opportunities and challenges that he accepted with faith.

Read of the path that molded his life, in which he is later labeled "the outstanding Grand Master on the North American continent." Learn of his tragedies and triumphs in mid-western Minnesota. He survived several life-threatening events and witnessed historic events when their impact was felt locally in midwestern Minnesota.

Share in the many experiences—socially, politically, religiously and financially—as Gordon Ekberg strives through the decades of life. Writing a column "Between the Cattails and the Bulrushes" for nearly 40 years for the American Pheasant and Waterfowl Society, Gordon conveyed the everyday life of lows and highs in a "folksy" way. You will want to experience reading his story of faith in God and compassion for his fellowman in spite of hardships. The scope of this book is endless and inspires the reader to grasp the fullness of life and to persevere.

At age four Gordon began to raise Rouen ducks, which led to a lifetime commitment to waterfowl and the environment. This passion expanded through the years as he raised 57 species of ducks, geese and swans from around the world.

His story, from 1933 to 2017 in midwestern Minnesota, shares his personal perspective set against the historical events of the day. As a teenager during World War II, Gordon repaired telephone lines and learned veterinary work to help the local community. Dropping out of school early in his junior year, which was traumatic for him as well as for his family, his further education continued through reading and experiences.

Gordon was active in lodge fellowship and speaking at church, where he developed his public speaking skills. He was exceptionally talented and intelligent; however, being an only child he felt the burden of his parents' hopes and dreams. At age 42, feeling he had let his parents down with no wife or family, he saw his future wife sitting in church. Married at age 43, another whole saga began that included art and the environment. Gordon's story inspires us to persevere and to educate ourselves through life-long learning as he entertains us with both wit and wisdom.

Gordon climbed the stairs for the last time (unbeknownst to him) on the evening of January 18, 2017, to see his manuscript of *Between the Cattails and the Bulrushes* sent to his editor, a historic moment in his life. He wanted to see his wife Gay "push the button" on the computer, sending an individual chapter with each click. Just several days later at Sanford Hospital with his wife and children by his side to comfort and support him through his final hours, the angels surrounded Gordon's hospital room waiting to take him to his eternal home.

With the approval of the Lake Region Arts Council to extend the Legacy Arts and Cultural Heritage Grant posthumously, the family has assumed the duties of working with editor Joy Minion and the printers, to complete his book, his dream, and to honor his precious memories as recorded in *Between the Cattails and the Bulrushes*.

— *Gay Ekberg, August 14, 2017*

Foreword

I have been going to write this book for years and have a difficult time getting started. Many people have urged me to write and there are so many things to consider: how to write? Use a computer, type or write in long hand? Each choice has its value, but here I am writing in long hand because of the convenience. It is so handy to have a legal pad on the kitchen or dining room table and a #2 pencil, with no electric cords to plug in. It seems that I can more easily convey my thought to the reader by writing… It is not easy to lead into something, so I will just bluntly write things as they come to me.

As a young boy, I was totally uninterested in joining anything: school, Sunday School, birthday parties—in fact any type of group activity. None of these things had any interest for me. I was an only child, and for the first six years of my life I was as close to being a child recluse as it as possible to be. My parents had the misfortune of losing my older brother and sister to infant death and so I was diligently cared for.

I am told that I could walk and talk at nine months, also learned to read at a fairly early age and was constantly inventing and making things—curiosity and imagination were very much a part of my makeup.

I went to school where I was the subject of extreme "bullying." During the first snowfall, I had my front tooth knocked out after I was "taken down" and given the option of either owning up to having a girl as my girlfriend or having my mouth packed full of the moist, wet snow— which I chose and was barely saved from choking to death.

So, life goes on... I terminated my high school education and became a "high school dropout" in my junior year. I worked hard at home, getting up at 4:30 a.m. to milk the cows. I also repaired telephone lines, helped with local veterinary efforts during World War II, and assumed leadership positions in a number organizations. It was both rewarding and otherwise; read about it in my book *Between the Cattails and the Bulrushes.*

— *Gordon Ekberg*
Lawndale Farm
November 2016

Contents

Before I Am

It Seems that the Milk is Sour

I was born at the end of the "roaring twenties" on June 18, 1929 in the beautiful, friendly and enterprising little town of Barrett, Minnesota. Few people would give a second thought to the possibility that I might have any connection to this lively little village. I have spent so little time in Barrett, nonetheless it was here that I struggled into this tough ol' world in the Powers Hospital. I say struggled because mine was a difficult birth effected by the use of instruments, which precipitated a broken shoulder blade and finally a squalling baby!

Before I am to be born, my parents had the sad and unnerving experience of having lost two babies about a year apart. First, a girl who did not survive because her cord was wrapped around her neck at birth. The second, a boy, who was born with an open spine and lived but two days.

It was unusual to be born in a hospital back in those days, but since my parents had lost my two older siblings during the birth process almost five years prior to my birth, they wanted to make every effort to ensure my safe arrival. Considering the harrowing events of my birthday, it was indeed most fortunate that they did so!

First and foremost, Dr. Fletcher W. Powers had earned the complete and utter confidence of my parents two years previously when my dad had a most serious accident. The damage to my father's left arm, which had been caught in the drive belt and drive pulley of a threshing machine, was extensive. It was so seriously mangled that the doctors from Herman and Elbow Lake, who had been called to Barrett to assist Dr. Powers in the serious emergency, immediately suggested amputation. Dr. Powers said, "No!" He was right. Although my father's left arm had been horribly mangled and broken in seven places, after much time and surgery it was once again a usable limb.

Second, Barrett was nearby and was an excellent facility, as well as being the only hospital in our county. Considering the excellent results on my father's arm, it was an easy choice for my folks to make for my birth. So I was born in Barrett and the fact that I never did live there has in no way diminished my enthusiasm and pride in the town!

Situated on the southwest shore of a little lake that produces good fishing as well as provides an excellent swimming beach, it's the frosting on the cake, indeed a beautiful spot! Its lakeside pavilion has hosted dances, political rallies and roller skating, as well as public and private family picnics and celebrations. The Roosevelt Hall, which is located uptown in the village of Barrett, was built during the Franklin Delano Roosevelt administration. It is the home base for the *Prairie Wind Players*, an excellent local theatre group that is quite active.

After my difficult birth, I had a very capable nurse, Mrs. Ben Olson, who cared for me in my first days of life. I wish I could say that I was a happy baby when I went home, but that was not the case. I was a very fussy baby and in fact lost weight every week. I was taken to a number of doctors in the area, but there seemed to be no help! My folks walked the floor with me in their arms to no avail! I cried all the time and seemed to be hurting. My parents did the only thing they knew, showed love by rocking me, holding me, and spending time with me. My mother rigged up a heavy cord string and pulley system that went from the kitchen to the dining room, where one end was tied to a very easy-to-rock, old time rocking chair that securely held my basket. From the kitchen, my mother would give a gentle tug on the string, which would start a gentle rocking motion. I would be quiet and Mom could get some work done, which otherwise was impossible.

As I look back on my fist weeks of life, I wonder how my folks held up after having lost my two siblings. I know it was a pretty serious situation from what Auntie Helen told me years later. She said it was heart-breaking for my mother who had lost two babies. She also had to deal with the very serious accident with my father's left arm that had hospitalized him for an extended period of time. Auntie related a day that had been especially bad when Grandpa Gord had been over so see me as we lived only about four miles apart. To auntie's inquiry about how I was doing, Grandpa told Auntie Helen most sorrowfully that, as much as he hated to say it, he was afraid that they were going to lose me just like the first two babies.

Grandpa Gord said that it was getting to him, too, to see me doing so poorly. It seemed at this point that few people around the neighborhood carried much hope for my survival. Grandpa was persistent and kept suggesting they try different doctors even though it seemed hopeless! He now came up with the name of a different doctor at Fergus Falls, which was 40 miles away. The name he suggested was Dr. Carl O. Estrem, who was an older doctor and was his cousin. Grandpa was so wanting to see me in Estrem's care that he went along with my folks when they took me to Fergus Falls.

I don't remember the events of the day but I was told afterwards that we all went into Dr. Estrem's office and after briefing the kindly doctor, he said to us all while looking at Grandpa Gord, "Well, Hank I shouldn't wonder but that some old-fashioned Norwegian *rømmegrøt* might do this boy some good. It's really not that simple, but he may be suffering from a lack of stomach acidity that he needs to digest his milk to get some food values and nutrients, because it appears to me that the boy is starving! Try this when you get home—take a bottle of fresh cow's milk, add a few drops of Lactic acid by means of an eye dropper, and either shake up or beat up the treated milk with an egg beater so that it is a very liquid consistency. Give the customary amount and put him down for a nap and we will see what happens."

Well, my folks were so surprised that they could hardly wait to get home and try what Dr. Estrem suggested—for it did not seem logical after the many medications that had been prescribed fruitlessly by doctors far and near, all to no avail. It just seemed far too simple. But they prepared the bottle as Dr. Estrem advised and noted a somewhat more enthusiastic nursing on the bottle, but not much. Auntie Helen, who had come along home with the folks, related this to me afterward that I was a different baby who awoke from the nap than had been put down. She said the very first feeding of sour milk worked like a miracle. I took to the sour milk like bees to honey. I perked up right away, and what rejoicing in the Ekberg household! Before long I no longer cried and instead smiled! Grandpa Gord was just so happy to see what a wonderful response his cousin Dr. Estrem's advice had effected. It was not long before the whole neighborhood was aware of what Dr. Estrem's wise, beneficial advice had accomplished! From then on I grew like a weed, until I reached my present 6 feet 2 inch stature. From then on the growth has been noted only in my waistline, and that doesn't appear to have the built in "hold" like my height.

It was a lesson for us all that in life, when some things "go sour," it doesn't mean it is bad! All my life I have enjoyed sour milk. When neighbor boys would stay overnight, they always mentioned my drinking sour milk. They said, "And you should hear him drink his milk through his teeth!" A most interesting noise as I "slurped" my milk! I still love the stuff after 86 years!

Gordon with his dad, Walter, peering into the baby basket.
The basket remains in the Ekberg home.

The Relatives

In Norway, Sweden and Here

Many writers have extended histories of their immigrant forbearers. I have a unique history of maternal grandparents. This is how this has come about. A relative, Elmer Nelson, and I have a common great-grandparent in Norway. About 50 years ago, Elmer was cleaning out his basement and ran across some old letters from Norway. He had a number of letters from the 1850s when my maternal grandfather, Henry Gaard, was making up his mind whether or not he would like to immigrate to America when he got old enough to do so. My grandfather was just a pre-teen boy at that time, but had been exposed to some of the realities of life with its hardships.

Anyway, Elmer had a number of copies and asked if I would like him to share the many letters from our great-grandparent, Ole Helgesonn Gaard, and having always been a history "nut," I said, "Yes." Elmer gave me eleven copies, and I thought way back then that I might try to write a book about my life and this would be something unique to include. I had read some immigrant pioneer histories, but they always began with the subject arriving at our shores. *Here,* I thought, i*s a chance for me to see what was going through my grandparents' (or any immigrant's) minds that would prompt them to leave home and family to start a new life in America.*

What I found out, and I don't mean this "lightly," is that I am here in the U.S.A. instead of being born in Norway because in the 1850s the herring in the North Sea fishing grounds where my grandfather's family did their herring fishing were getting progressively smaller each year. In other words, fishing—both in volume and quality—was getting poorer each year. It apparently looked to my great-grandfather Ole that his son, my Grandpa Henry (originally spelled *Helge*), would make a good choice by coming to this country. I somewhat lightly say that I am living here in the U.S.A. because the herring fishing was getting progressively poorer in the 1850s in the North Sea. It brings a smile, but it's true.

There were also other factors that my grandfather listed. Great-grandfather Ole was a well-educated man and had a good position in the Bank of Norway near Haugesund. I have found my great-grandfather's writings to be of substance, very revealing and most interesting to help others understand just why there are so many immigrants in this country.

My great-grandfather Ole was a man of substance, being appointed to the Royal Apportionment Commission in his area as well as serving as Mayor and being among those who started The Savings Bank in the Torvestad and Skaare area. His letters to his children, three of whom immigrated to Minnesota, are most interesting.

I have further insight into the Depression and the Franklin Delano Roosevelt Administration because my uncle, Irven R. Ekberg, was one of 17 field men who supervised the activities of Roosevelt's Administration Agriculture Adjustment Act of the 1930s. He too had interesting stories to tell.

In addition, my paternal grandfather, Frank Ekberg, served as a County Commissioner for the county and knew Minnesota's James J. Hill, the Empire Builder.

Also, my own father, Walter C. Ekberg, served on and promoted the local co-op elevator board, was on the local creamery board as well as helped organize the Herman Locker Plant. He was a successful farmer known for good farming practices, and was one of the first large cattle feeders in the state.

All of this, plus my wife and I along with our children made a significant contribution to art in our area. My wife has served on the Lakes Region Arts Council and we have a wildlife art gallery on the farm. We have sponsored major artists many times, with their art shows often being attended by over 300 people who were exposed to the impressive professionals in art. Our efforts in the art world continue and have spanned over 30 years. Also, we have made efforts on behalf of the National Farmers Organization (NFO) and the Lawndale Environmental Foundation, Inc.

Below: Letter from Great-grandfather Ole

Gaard, 8th March 1885.

To Endre Sigbjørnsen

Your letter of February 9th I got yesterday. I now will tell you something from here. We are all with good health up to this time. We now have been a litle out fishing hering. I amd Tollef, Hans-Ole og and Bendik Østrem, we are together. We were 5 days in Røvær, from the 17th to the 21st of Fegruary, but it was merely good hopes there and nothing else. Much whale, no netfishing, but some small seines with very litle fish. The outlooks were diminished every day. Saturday we had good weather and then we turned home 60 coalfish and 13 herings was what/ we got on that trip. Sunday we got a big storm from south-east with snow. Stronger storm we have not had the last 20 years. At home we lost half a hundred pans from the roof. Monday the weather was better again with a litle rain, so that the snow almost disappeard. Sunday there was a sailing wessel on the Flakket og or Flæ outside Suggevaagen in Røvær, and this boat was taken by the storm. The cable broke. It was a good boat, one of the american fishing-boats that came from the eastern part of Norway. The boat lay there in Røvær with the fishermen on board. Twelve men were on board. In the evening the boat turned round. Wednesday it drifted on the shore near Buelandet 10 miles north of Bergen. Fiwe men were dead and seven in a bad condition, as they had been on board the dammaged boat for so long a time. Stormy weather with rain it was almost every day that week. Friday and saturday most of the fishermen came home from Røvær. The storm the said saturday, dammaged the breakwater-mole in three places in the southern bay in Sira. The week from the 1st to the 7th of March the weather has been good. Tuesday the 3rd of March they closed a fish in nets in Røvær and also some in Smørsund.
In Røvær there were not many peoples, and there it was no fishing either, but in Smørsund and Ramsholmen, and also at the islands Loddersy, there has been good fishing the whole week, especially bottomfishing. Manu whales have been here every day the whole week in the district between Tømmer-hammer and Lyngholmen, and west to the Bleiskjærene. But near the mainland there has not been hering, except outside Smørsund. In Norderne there has also been a litle fishing this week. The hering is fine and big springhering. The price has been very low, about 4 Kroner a barrel. Mathias came from Sira saturday the 28th of February . They then finished. They earned a litle more than 40 Kroner each. Tuesday last week we went north to Mølstrevaag. Mathias took tollefs place. We havn't made any good fishing, but we have got plenty of hering for our own use, about 3 or 4 barrels, and a litle we have sold also at the price of 5 Kroner the barrel. Yesterday I was in the Consiliating Board. There were 56 agreementsfor the bank and 3 other compromises. In Haugesund it is bad with the banking business and also other business it seems. The Haugesund bank was betrayed for, or it was stolen, 42.000 Kroner by a boy that worked for the bank. He has now been arrested. The Skillingsbank or Sparekassen has gone bankrupt, and they say that it will give 50% at most. The directors have been shown out of the bank, and two other men have been taken in to do their work. Loans no one can get. Ingebret Storesund and his son have gone bankrupt. Hans Stensnes and Kolbein Sund, watkhmaker Olsen and Børseth will be bank-rupt very soon. The bookseller Salte has closed, and how many more I can not tell. Lauritz Pettersen I think also will have to finish.

~ 7 ~

My Grandpa Henry left his home in Norway consisting of his parents, Ole and Anna, and his brothers and sisters. He was never able to return again, not even for the visit he dreamed of. When he came to America, he changed the spelling of his name from Gaard to Gord.

He met my grandmother, Anna Knutsen, while he sailed the Great Lakes. They were married and lived in Milwaukee, Wisconsin, and had three children: My mother Adell Konvally (aka Della), Frank Oneal, and Helen Edna. Frank died of tuberculosis at the age of two, and a short time later my grandmother contracted tuberculosis and died at the age of 29. Grandpa had the help of a kindly neighbor couple, Mr. and Mrs. B.A. Lenvick, for some time. Eventually, he sent his two daughters, my mother and her little sister, to make their home at Elbow Lake, Minnesota, with his sister Helen and her husband, E.S. Nelson.

Grandpa Henry was farming in the Herman area by the time my mother was about 11 years old. The thrill of owning their own farm was short-lived. They had a good crop of potatoes that year, and because of some low land that retained moisture the potatoes were very good. It was a totally unexpected surprise that with the potato sales and a few other things, there was enough money to pay off the mortgage on the farm. The check was written out to the mortgage company in Breckenridge, a town 40 miles away. The family was so happy they had tears in their eyes. After all that hard work and sacrifice they owned a farm.

Unfortunately, the Grant County State Bank of Herman, on which the final check was drawn to pay off the mortgage, closed its doors and declared bankruptcy while my grandfather's check was in transit. The outcome was that the farm was claimed by the Mortgage Company.

Thus, Grandpa developed an angina pectoris heart condition. For a time Grandpa and Auntie Helen moved in with us until they could find a vacant farmhouse to rent. Once settled in at their rented farm, Grandpa started to make me a Christmas present out of scrap lumber and apple boxes. It was a masterful piece, a wonderful toy barn that those gnarled hands made, fashioning this gift with skill and love. There were animals and poultry carved from bits and pieces of scrap lumber. All of it looked so life-like that I was completely captivated by it! It was the only present that I had eyes for. My mother told me years afterwards that the way my eyes shone and the attention I gave my barn left no doubt in anyone's mind that I really liked the barnyard layout and had made my Grandpa so happy! I still have the barn today. It has stood the test of time, even after having been played with by my children and grandchildren. I got it Christmas Eve in 1934. I remember the details of that night as though it were yesterday.

The events of that Christmas season were memorable for another reason. We had been to Grandpa and Grandma Ekberg's for Christmas Day dinner and had come home in the evening, had done the milking, after chores had a light lunch, and had gone to bed early. We were all asleep and at about 10 o'clock the phone rang with the alarming news that Grandpa Gord, who just the night before had given me the toy barnyard, had died of a heart attack. He and Auntie Helen had been to his brother's family home for Christmas Day and had left for home on the slightly blustery night and had gotten stuck in a small snow drift. Grandpa got out to push the car while Auntie tried to drive ahead. Pushing was something he had been told not to do, but the drift was so small, he thought this little bit this once shouldn't matter. He pushed the car out and got back in the driver's seat and slumped over, dead. This five-year-old child had a really tough time trying to comprehend death.

My dad got up and got dressed after calling upstairs to the hired man to come along. I took the opportunity to crawl into bed with my mother and comfort her while Dad and the hired man were gone. My mind was apparently on how to make Grandpa well, because my suggestion to my mother was that Dad should take a small jar of Vicks® VapoRub™ to heal Grandpa. My reasoning was based on the fact that whenever I got sick or had a cold, out came the Vicks®, which was rubbed on my chest followed by a warm flannel rag and a hot water bottle to complete the treatment. The Vicks® treatment plus hot lemonade usually produced successful results by morning. I was sure that it would do the same for Grandpa.

Mom tearfully tried to explain that death was different and that Grandpa had gone to Heaven.

Where is Heaven? How long will he be gone?

Mom said he was not coming back.

Why not? Never, EVER? Never, EVER? Then I wanted to know just where Heaven was.

Mom said, "Up in the sky among the stars."

"Well, which stars?" I persisted. *Could she point them out? Could Grandpa see us down here? Could we wave to him?* My first awareness of death left a lasting impression. It was incomprehensible that my beloved "Bop Poo" as I called him, who just the night before had given me the wonderful barn, wasn't coming back to play with me, never, ever.

Also, that same Christmas Eve that I got my barn we played an old Norwegian Folk game taught by my Grandpa Gord. All the rest of the guests had gone home. Grandpa and Grandma Ekberg, Aunt Effie, Uncle Irven and Aunt Charlotte Ekberg and their daughters had left. There were just five of us playing the game: Mom, Dad, Auntie Helen, Grandpa, and me. Grandpa Gord was "it" and sat on a chair within the small pen made by laying the kitchen chairs on their sides on the floor in the corner of the kitchen. In the pen were all the overshoes from those of us who were still participating. The object was for the rest of us to try to steal a pig, represented by the overshoes. Grandpa was the farmer who would hit with a club if someone tried to steal a "pig." The club was actually a long everyday stocking with something soft poked down into the toe. The object was to steal a pig without getting hit by the "club." What an exciting game and what fun we had! The night's finale was Grandpa leading us around the house while beating to the march time on a toy drum that I also got that night. When the march was over, Grandpa and Auntie went home. What an evening, such fun! It was just like it was supposed to be like that! Everyone enjoyed everything! Grandpa was in his glory because I so loved the barn and had such a good time. He, of course, never came back. Grampa Gord was 68 years old when he died.

Other remembrances come to mind. Grandpa Gord liked to tease me. I hate to have my face washed and as soon as we got to the sink he would caution, "Don't 'wet' the nose!" And as soon as that was said, I would dive right in and get my whole face wet!

THE SWEDEN FOLKS

My Grampa Frank Ekberg came to stay with us after his wife Augusta passed away. They were living at Herman in a home that stood on the corner where the *Herman Review* now stands. Grandpa Ekberg requested that he come back to this farm home where he had raised his family, to live with us. He had built this house and had specifically built the stairs with easy rising steps, an open stairway with a landing, so that he would always be able to walk up it, even in old age. My mom Della was patient with him—typical of older people, he wanted things done "right now." Like taking care of the garden "now." In his last months with us, he became bedridden and needed the help of an area caregiver, Mrs. Charlotte Corcoran, a devout Catholic who was the mother of 13 children. She was a wonderful help. My mom continued with extensive laundry duties without the benefit of a modern washing machine. Again, she was a patient person.

Grandpa Ekberg was the son of my great grandparents Isaak and Johana (Gustafson) Ekberg, who were born and married in Sweden. Isaak was born in 1828 at Traheryd, Smaland, Sweden. This couple originally arrived in St. Paul, where Isaak worked in the carpenter trade. Later they moved to Herman, where Isaak worked for the Great Northern Railway Company and eventually took a 160-acre homestead in Macsville township. They had four children: Frank Albert, Gustaf Ferdinand, Carl Victor, and a sister recalled as "Mrs. Peter Noreen." This was their home until he passed in 1916 at the age of 87 years; his wife continued living there. He was an early settler, living here for 40 years, and was very active in the civic life of Macsville. He was a charter member of the Swedish Lutheran Church in Herman. Both he and his family were highly regarded in the social and religious life of his district.

Grandpa Ekberg was educated in both Sweden and in Herman, moving to the United States at the age of 12 years in 1875. He also took 160 acres in section 14 of Macsville, planted a grove of trees, and eventually built substantial buildings where he farmed and raised stock until 1900. Frank sold his father Isaak's farm in 1899 (known more recently as the "Gilbertson place.") In 1900 he moved to the present farm site, which was 360 acres in section 3, a piece he had purchased in 1896. Here he planted a large grove, built "modern" buildings, and again engaged in farming and raising stock (a fine herd of shorthorn cattle.) He also was active in civic affairs, as county commissioner and on the school board (for 25 years.) He was a representative to state political conventions several times, being recognized as a leader in his party.

Frank married Augusta Wilhelmena Peterson in 1885. She was also born in Sweden (1864) and her parents were Peter Otto and Johanna Peterson, who had come to Minnesota in 1880 and located in Herman. Frank and Augusta had five children: Oscar Albert, Effie Annetta, Walter Clay, Irven Richard and Ray Conrad. Frank was recognized as one of the most systematic and successful farmers in the county, also being progressive as a public official and accomplishing much good. His home place was one of the most beautiful places in the community, kept neat and well maintained.

My dad, Walter, was the one to continue living and farming on the "home place." I was fortunate also to grow up and raise my five children here in the house built in 1900. My wife Gay and I decided to take up the name of the farm, as initially named by Grandpa Ekberg, Lawndale Farm, to honor him and the "home place." With some restoration of new windows and doors, we are able to live in and enjoy the home we have shared for 44 years.

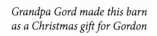

Grandpa Gord made this barn
as a Christmas gift for Gordon

The Storm at Barrett Lake

The beautiful little lake next to Barrett, Minnesota, has so captivated me through the years. Ironically, it almost claimed my life during those early years. It happened like this.

June 24 was one of those holidays that rated a celebration in Barrett, a day in which there were gatherings, rallies, political speeches, reunions, picnics, dances, carnivals and boat rides. It was a possibility of a boat ride that claimed this four-year-old boy's attention. Now this was to be no ordinary boat ride. It was to be on the Hjelle brothers' steam launch, and it was **big** to my way of thinking. It was 36 feet long with a canvas top and a smoke stack that puffed real smoke. I begged and teased for a ride all day long. It had been a busy day for those running the boat and giving rides.

Finally, my dad decided we could go. Dusk was falling, but no matter—the boat had a strong headlight. As it docked right below the pavilion, those who had completed their ride got off and those waiting to take a ride (like my dad and me) were getting on. My mother was there to see us off, along with her sister, Auntie Helen, and her father, Grandpa Henry Gord. It was an awesome sight to see this big boat pull up to the dock and let off and then load passengers.

When loaded, the boat majestically moved away from the dock and headed for a nice long ride to the northwest corner of the lake. *The longer the better*, I thought in eager anticipation. Then the wind seemed to come up slightly and slowly. In fact, it was almost imperceptible. The sky seemed to darken, but the engineer's confidence seemed to be in the big boat—even though the passengers made suggestions to turn back to the dock. Full steam to the furthest corner of the lake appeared to be foremost in the engineer's mind. Winds were picking up and it was starting to rain. Rain and wind were coming harder and faster, and pleas to turn back were the order of the day as fear ran rampant. Some passengers were crying and screaming as the boat took on water. Turning the boat in such high waves was really risky business. Water was splashing over the railings. Finally, the engineer snapped the boat around and we were on our way back to the dock at the pavilion.

Running with the wind! The high waves made it almost impossible to dock. The engine was getting wet and controlling the boat was a real problem. My dad jumped over the side into water almost up to his neck. The engineer lifted me up and set me on my dad's shoulders, which were often covered with water as the tempest sloshed him back and forth. I was scared half to death that my dad would be knocked off his feet and this four year old little boy with him, but we finally got to shore and into the open arms of my mother and Auntie and Grandpa Gord. Those waiting agonizingly on shore were as cold and wet as Dad and me. How thankful we all were!

I'd had hopes of a getting a hamburger at the Anderson Café in downtown Barrett that day, but the folks were so grateful to have Dad and me safe that they wanted to get me home, warmed up and dried off as soon as possible. And so the anticipation of the hamburger following the boat ride faded rather rapidly into oblivion. It was so special, not only the hamburger, but the café. The Anderson Café was so different. Just like two buildings in one. On one side was the pool hall and beer parlor, and on the other side was the restaurant where meals were served. While at that age I did not spend much time in pool halls, it seemed so special to walk through the big double doors going into the pool hall and the restaurant. Well, there would be other times.

The days and weeks that followed were hot and dirty, the dust bowl was moving in along with the tumbling "tumbleweeds" (Russian thistle.) So thick were the dust storms that the sky was darkened and day was actually turned into night. My dad and the hired men came in from the fields because they couldn't see where they were going! The crops were so poor that there was little for the livestock to eat. Hog wire fencing was put around hayracks so we wouldn't lose so much hay and also so we could cut the round tumbleweeds and haul them home to put them through the silage cutter and make silage. It turned out to be pretty fair feed.

The tumbleweeds were round like large beach balls and when they were ripe the roots would release them from the ground and they would roll across the countryside spreading their seed for next year. The wire fencing around the hayracks kept the wind from lifting the tumbleweeds off the rack. The musical group, The Sons of the Pioneers, glorified the tumbleweeds with their song, *Tumbling Tumbleweeds*. The song was a hit and a good one, but what it stood for—hard times, dust storms, starving livestock, farmers going broke, and heartbroken people having to leave their homes—was not good.

SURVIVING THE STORM, I SURVIVE TO BECOME A WRITER:

My writing in the *American Pheasant and Waterfowl Society Magazine* (*APWS Magazine*) has gone around the world—even to Oxford University in England, which subscribes to it at their library. Consequently, I had a gentleman call me whose home was in Connecticut—he said that he read my article in the *APWS Magazine* in Oxford University in England. He was home on a summer furlough from there and said that it was amazing to see the readership we had there. He wanted some advice on raising cygnets (young swans.)

But before that, he asked, "Is it true that you are a high school drop out?"

And I said, "Yes."

"Over at Oxford we marvel as we read your columns that they are so substantially interesting and free of errors. But what I would really like to know is how to feed a young swan."

I told him, "You could give the young swan commercial chick feed that is possibly up to 28-30% protein, or you could let the parent birds raise them if you have a pond in front of your place where they could harvest their own water bugs, crustaceans and the like, as well as plants in the case of swans."

Then he asked if this was readily available in all ponds.

"Yes, possibly in the bottom of a five-foot-deep pond."

He asked, "How will the little cygnets get this?"

I told him that our Creator arranged for the parent swans to gather the little ones around them while the male strenuously paddled in place, causing a current to sweep up from the bottom all of the delicacies of that underworld for nourishing swans.

So this is how I found out that our readership includes one of the world's leading universities.

Trumpeter Swans at Lawndale Farm

Close Calls
On My Life

Many years ago I had resolved to write a book about my life, and finally in the last few years began to slowly but surely start to see this materialize. At first, I thought I could never fill a book with experiences out of my life history that would be interesting enough for others to want to read—I thought my life was too ordinary, too mundane. However, after getting started many memories flashed through my mind. I am putting down some of the close calls on my life, indicating, I believe, that God was saving me to write this book, *Between the Cattails and the Bulrushes*. This chapter is about some of the more frightening events that stood out in my mind.

In those early days, all of us farmers would thresh a large straw pile of small grain in the livestock yard for the cattle when they were kept off their pasture in the non-growing season of the year. This pile also furnished a rather limited shelter from the colder weather. This feed supply of light grain and weed seeds, as well as choice straw, was of lesser nutrition than hay.

One of our young shorthorn cows had a calf outside the barn in the early chill by the shelter of the straw pile. I was about two or three years of age and had been told not to try to see the calf except in the company of an adult. Why? Because the young mother cow was very protective of the newborn calf and did not want anyone or anything to come near. Well, that warning to me at that age was soon forgotten.

At the time, no one had the time to take me to see the calf so I took it upon myself to toddle down to the livestock yard. I crawled under the gate and walked down to the straw pile, where the cow promptly discovered me. With a bellow and a snort, she charged at me with all the fury that a mother cow could muster when her calf was approached by this new creature, me. Our dog, thank God, had accompanied me or I would have been a "goner." The cow was trying to defend her calf from me and the dog, and the dog was trying to defend me from the charging cow.

I had run for the gate at the first move of the cow, but never could have made it under the gate as two barbed wires caught my clothes, preventing me from easily exiting the livestock yard. At that moment, my father appeared and frantically rescued me.

The next close call was a few years later on Armistice Day, November 11, 1940. Besides being a commemoration of when the first World War ended, years later this event was referred to as the date of the worst snowstorm (Storm of the Century), when many people had lost their lives.

It was also the furbearing and small game season, which included muskrat trapping. I had a number of traps set on Johnson Lake, which we rented for our extended pasture in the summer. A number of muskrat houses were visible out on the frozen lake. The price of the furs averaged around a dollar and half per pelt, and that was pretty good money back in those days. I had a number of traps set that had to be checked morning and night. If a muskrat had gotten in the trap, it could very possibly chew its leg off and get away if not checked in time. Well, I did not want any to get away so I checked my traps both morning and night, and I was being rewarded for catching some muskrats—good money for an 11-year-old boy. On this particular day, I made the most of the opportunity by riding my pony, Polly, the mile to Johnson Lake.

It was a beautiful spring-like day when I left home riding bareback on my pony, because the 90-pound saddle was too heavy for this 11-year-old boy to lift onto her back. I would live to regret that decision.

I dressed rather lightly because it was such a beautiful warm day—no need to dress warmer than necessary. I left home on my pony early to be out on the lake before 8 a.m. I tied her to an old fallen tree for two reasons. First, because it was the thing to do. Second, because I did not have a saddle on her, I would need assistance to get back on; by tying her close to the fallen tree, I could use it as kind of a ladder to get on her back. I had with me a burlap gunny sack in which to place the muskrats after I caught and killed them.

The beautiful morning was materializing into a wonderful day, with bright sunshine and not a cloud in the sky, and only a slight breeze out of the northwest. I was so absorbed in catching muskrats and it was such a glorious day—but then something got my attention. I thought I felt snowflakes hit my cheeks! I hadn't noticed that the sun had gone under a cloud—it was snowing and getting colder. Still, that didn't alarm me because I had been out in snowstorms before. However, this was happening so fast.

All of a sudden, I could not see my pony only 25 feet away on the shore of the lake. All of a sudden I was so scared; the snow was sticking to my face and my eyelids were freezing. My pony was restless. I had better hit for home. Now, the snow was coming faster and I was starting to panic. I was having trouble calming my pony, and more trouble getting on her back. I started to cry and that didn't help. What to do. I had to stop everything and assess the situation. More than anything, I needed to keep calm.

This was important because I was in pastures that were laid out like kind of a maze and with the escalating tempo of the storm, I could see neither landmarks nor trail. I had to formulate in my mind the path to get out. There would be serious consequences if I was caught in the pasture.

The first hazard was the fact that we had to ride head first into the northwest wind to get home, and my pony had a way of turning her back to the wind—just the opposite direction from which I wanted to go. She did not want to face the wind. It was really an effort to get her going in the right direction. Finally, I got her headed toward what I thought was home. At last I held the reigns up and let the pony choose the trail. After about half an hour she stopped—we were up against a barbed wire fence. Where were we?

There was a gate in this maze, which caused me to panic; I could not get off the pony to open the gate because there was no dead tree to help me get back on her. I had to open the gate without getting off. More than once I almost slipped off her back. After we finally got through the gate, she seemed more aggressive and I took that to mean we were getting closer to home. Sure enough, after about another 15 minutes my pony stopped and refused to go any further. Thank God, to whom I had been praying to all the time! I could vaguely make out the shape of the barn. We were home!

I could dimly make out the barn door, which was now opening. A man came out. He had been peering through a 10-inch by 12-inch window in case I should miraculously get home. The man was Zibe Danzeisen, who worked for us at the time. He lifted me off the pony—I was cold and every bit as stiff as a statue. I could not walk so Zibe carried me to the house where he put me into my mother's arms. Her face was tear-stained—she thought she'd never see me again.

I was put in the bathtub fully clothed and allowed to warm up slowly. It was considered a miracle that an 11-year-old boy who had been out in the "Storm of the Century" for about two hours and covered four round-about miles had made it home! The prayers and my pony had done it. What a miracle!

My next close call came six years later when I was 17 years old. I had decided that I'd had enough experience doing welding so I embarked on making my own powered motor scooter. This was quite a job, as I soon found out. I worked long hours both early in the morning and late at night. We had a 300-amp electric welder that I had mastered, and I thought it really would be about all the special equipment I would need. Foolish boy! It turned out to be much more.

I was using the welder to heat up some rather heavy substantial irons to a red hot glow prior to bending them to my needs. I used a shop vise to hold the iron being bent and had the ground wire from the welder attached to the vise. Somehow, I was going to adjust the iron being bent so I could make the shape necessary to accomplish my purpose. When my hand went to the handle there was a loud "SNAP!" caused by a short in the welder. I was inadvertently, firmly and frightfully attached to the vise, which now allowed the vibrating current to course through my body. I could neither move nor speak as the painful current vibrated through me and most effectively incapacitated me. What to do. I could neither move nor yell; try as I would, nothing would function. I was paralyzed. I was frantically praying to God for deliverance, but to no avail.

Then my father walked nonchalantly in and almost immediately saw what was happening. I was momentarily relieved at the apparent help, until I saw that he was going to grab me in an effort to pull me off the vise. Horrors! If he touched me, we would both be doomed to death by electrocution. I tried to scream to warn him not to touch me, but no sound came out and at the last second before he reached me it dawned on him what the consequence would be if we touched. He then grabbed up a four-foot-long piece of a 2x6, a nonconductor of electricity, which he used to push me away from the vise. With great effort my father dislodged me from the vise and I fell to the ground barely conscious. Then using the piece of wood he maneuvered the electrical switch to the OFF position on the welding machine. We thanked God and called the doctor, who said the welding machine had been shorted in such a manner that no damage had been done to my heart and that all was well and life could continue. With profuse thanks to God, life did indeed go on. What an unforgettable experience!

You would think the memory of that horrible occasion would be etched very much on my mind—but don't you know, time dimmed the remembrance. About five years later, almost the same thing happened at harvest time. On a Sunday afternoon, the universal on the grain truck that runs the hoist came loose and had to be welded securely. I was home alone and it was not a very big job. The folks had gone to the Grant County Fair at Herman. I thought I could pull the truck that had almost a full load of barley up close to the machine shop where the welding cables would reach. I would have the thing welded, the balance of the barley unloaded and be combining again before the folks got home. It sounded good in my mind, so I proceeded with the plan.

Now you understand that this was the same welding machine that had malfunctioned a couple of years previously—except that I'd had the welding machine overhauled by a qualified electrician, who pronounced it being as good as new. Yet I still took many precautions, such as wearing rubber boots so I would not get grounded to the machine. I took even further precautions by wearing rubber gloves with rubber gauntlets attached that protected my arms just up to my elbows. It seemed like I had used every possible precaution.

Well, I got the truck up to the shop and got a "crawler" so that I could crawl on my back under the truck and be comfortably close to the welding site. After pulling on all the rubber paraphernalia, I turned the welding machine on and crawled under the truck. I started to weld and the repair was going nicely. I was feeling quite proud of myself.

I rechecked the welding job and it seemed good. I thought maybe the other side of the weld should be checked, so I reached over my head to turn the shaft being welded. I didn't notice that the gauntlet had slid down and my bare arm somehow made contact with the metal part of the truck. Trying to shift my positon, I found myself being electrocuted by what had been a normally-functioning machine. There was no way to get loose!

I was terrified as I prayed to God for forgiveness for working on Sunday. I struggled to get loose; if not, would God please receive me into His Kingdom? As I committed myself to God, I dropped off the truck! Was I ever thankful!

These incidents are some of the many times I have had close calls with death and miracles happened. I am hoping to finish this book!

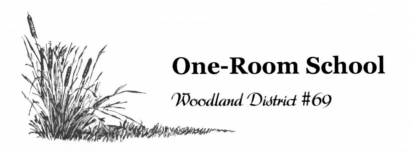

One-Room School
Woodland District #69

My first recollection of school was when one of our neighbors asked my mother one day, "Well, I suppose this young man starts school this spring?"

My mother acknowledged that to be true. The days were getting longer and the days were getting warmer with spring and the start of two months of kindergarten. This would be my introduction to the philosophy of education and really life itself. School days were rapidly approaching. How was I going to be prepared for that? I was loaded with questions about what it was, when, how often did I have to go and where.

I remember the day my dad brought home a new lunch bucket, not the only school purchase, but the one I remember the most. He brought it home in the old farm truck. The lunch bucket was rectangular with two handles that met on the top. It was about four inches deep and was painted in a beautiful green scotch plaid pattern with gold and black accent lines. It contained a thermos bottle to carry soup or possibly hot cocoa. I visualized the soup and how nice that would be, but my delight was short-lived.

None of the other kids had anything that elaborate and so they made fun of it. I liked the lunch box but not the thermos because it apparently smacked of being a sissy-type item. I did not want to be different! Needless to say, it took a long time before I could be induced to take the thermos to school. By then some of the other kids were using them too. My dad felt bad, still I went to school for some time minus the thermos. The first day of school, I had been exposed to peer pressure! Life's constant companion!

I went to a one-room country school, which had a total of 28 students when I started kindergarten. "As the crow flies" it was less than half mile from my home to Woodland, District #69, grades K-8. It was staffed by a solitary teacher, who also acted as custodian, school nurse, playground supervisor, etc.

The school day began at 9 a.m. and let out at 4 p.m., five days a week. Most kids started arriving at 8:30, not only to get in on game playing but also to do daily assigned chores such as carrying water from the well in water pails for the drinking water, which was drunk from a common dipper shared by all! After a few years we did get a portable stone crock that had an overflow that went into a water pail if the water missed the kids' mouths. That pail of water was then used for cleaning purposes. Another daily chore was to carry in the coal or wood to the big box for the stove. There was also the daily chore of sweeping the outdoor toilets, which like all the tasks were assigned to teams of two and alternated every other week.

Teachers usually spent only two to four years in a school and then moved on. The theory seemed to be that by changing teachers, there was an opportunity to expose the students to varying abilities and expertise. The curriculum was arranged so that we were exposed to all the basics, plus specific classes to enhance them. The superintendent visited each school in session every four to five weeks to see all were achieving a stable and acceptable level of learning. I felt we had received an excellent, well-rounded education in the old one-room school I attended.

In my grade level there was only one other student, a neighbor girl, Joan Mae Johnson. After a couple years, others joined us, a boy and a girl: Earl Ray Danzeisen moved down here from Canada and Arlene Wirtjes moved in from outside the district. Both brought with them two siblings. Earl, whom we called Ray (his middle name), brought an older brother Orville Jay Danzeisen and a younger brother LeRoy. Arlene Wirtjes brought two younger siblings, Arnold and Dorothy. They moved into the far side of the district on farms within a half mile of each other, so they alternated sharing rides to school. Both Ray and Arlene were a nice addition to our class, which numbered four by the time we were in the third or fourth grade when we were learning to perfect our reading with the use of phonics.

In our earlier grades, we learned to read by using *Dick and Jane* books and on through *Tom and Betty* books. We also read *The Three Bears* and *The Three Billy Goats Gruff*, which we acted out. I thought that was fun, especially when Goldilocks was found in the baby bear's bed and when the bridge was in danger of collapse with the conflict between the three goats and the troll.

How did I get to school? When I started kindergarten, my parents took me in a car, or sometimes in the winter when the roads were bad we went in the bobsled pulled by a team of horses. Otherwise I walked, which was about a mile.

Our class sessions were broken up by recesses. There were three recesses a day: two 15-minute recesses held halfway through the morning and afternoon, and a one-hour recess at noon from noon until one o'clock. On nice days we went outside during recess and played games: kitten ball, football with no helmets, and ante-over-the-woodshed. The boys generally played cops and robbers while the girls played games such as drop the handkerchief or went on walks. We also played games where the whole school was involved, such as Dare Base, Pump-Pump-Pull-Away, and Kick the Can.

When it rained or snowed or we had unseasonable weather, we stayed in the school building and played indoor games such as Hangman, To the Mill and Back, and Tic, Tac Toe. We also played Musical Chairs and Clap 'em In and Clap 'em Out.

There is so much being said about bullying now, but it was no different when I went to school. Bullying took many forms, from just plain teasing to most boys having their pants taken down or taken off and humiliated in that manner, just being exposed. Some kids were teased and bullied to tears. I had snow shoved in my mouth until I nearly suffocated, trying to get me to say what they wanted to hear. Fortunately, one friend intervened and probably saved my life. The poor teacher had such a work load that it was hardly possible for her to police the playground at all times! I don't think this was unique to our country school, because years later when we got to high school, boys who had attended other schools volunteered that similar humiliations had happened to them. Unless a child had older siblings, he was sure to be picked on. I had no siblings.

The bullying continued. As a six-year-old kindergartener, I had my ears severely pulled by the teacher as punishment for slapping a classmate, which I had been prodded to do by the older students. I was further punished by the teacher by being ordered outside all by myself into some most inclement rainy weather while the rest of the kids stayed inside. I still remember pulling on my boots in the entry and sobbing violently while the teacher stood over me with a ruler in hand, explaining that my father had said in a confrontation with her that he did not want to hear of me being confined when other kids were enjoying recess. That was in reference to an earlier occasion when the others were outside playing and I'd been kept inside as punishment.

Our schoolhouse sat up on cement blocks and in later years a cement foundation was poured. Unfortunately, the reoccurring problem of a skunk taking up residence under the building continued. Although the cement foundation was intended to remedy the problem, the structure was compromised by the addition of two ¼-inch, screened galvanized windows on each end of the building. Their purpose was to allow airflow so the building would be rid of any musty, moldy smell.

However, some of the kids skillfully loosened the screened windows and deceptively camouflaged the area. The idea was to entice the skunk family to return so that some ingenious young man could come to school early some morning, poke his rat terrier dog through the hole, and wait until the confrontation took place, the skunk being "trigged." The desired response was to have the stench of the skunk be so repulsive that school would be cancelled for the day! The school board came and after a great deal of effort solved the problem. Previously, the smell had been vented out more readily through the open blocks.

Our school rouser was composed by classmate Milton Lueneburg:

Woodland, Woodland, Invincible 69
We're off to victory in a game of any kind!
And when you're up against us
We'll sweep you off your feet,
And in your eyes you'll realize that,
A Woodlander can't be beat!

Gordon's school days photo

Gordon's classmates from the country school in Macsville Township.
Ray Danzeisen, Rudy Raths and Milton Lueneberg continued a lifelong friendship,
visiting whenever they could or exchanging Christmas cards.

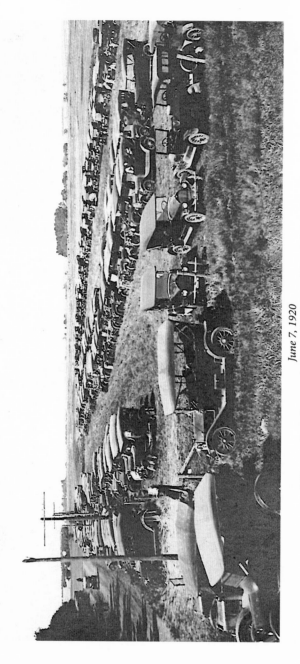

June 7, 1920
A Non-partisan League picnic was held at neighbor Halvar Johnson's
home. Over 1,200 cars parked in the field behind the grove.
The country school in Macsville Township was located
at the east edge of Johnson's home site.

Mr. Button and
the Big Horse

Usually a farmer would breed a mare or two in the spring of the year, anticipating a colt 11 months later. While every farm had a male sheep (ram), male cattle (bull), or male hog (boar), most everyone did not own a male horse (stallion). Why? Because they were too aggressive and hard to handle. What to do? Well, what to do—a group of farmers went together and purchased a registered purebred stallion and hired a man to drive around the countryside with the communal stallion and breed the designated mares. In other words, they founded a joint stallion club.

In our case, the club had purchased a fine registered Percheron stallion and hired a rather elderly gentleman to have charge of the stallion and service the mares in our area. For our area, this was Mr. Albert Belding. As a small boy around four years old, I could not pronounce the name Belding and so I called him Mr. Button. I had a rather interesting time when Mr. Button came to our place to see if one of our mares was ready for service.

Now, as a small boy I had no idea what the real purpose of Mr. Button's business really was. I think the term was "visiting," and I was totally innocent and unaware of the true purpose of the visit. This rather interesting event was scheduled to take place out behind the barn, where I was not allowed to watch.

There was a great deal to see and hear, which really got this little boy's curiosity. I had seen Mr. Button coming around the lake and went to meet him with the hopes of getting a ride on his cart behind the big horse. Sure enough, Mr. Button obliged by finding a place on the seat of the cart for me to ride the approximate quarter of a mile up to our yard.

As I said before, there was a lot to see and hear and my curiosity was aroused first of all by the big horse that arrived with Mr. Belding. It announced its presence in my neighborhood by way of greeting with a whinny. It could easily be heard a half mile away and could be called a scream. It was most impressive and would leave no doubt in anyone's mind that something special was about to occur. I was not allowed to witness the event, whatever it might be. After our mare and the stallion, together with Mr. Button, my father and the hired man, were behind the barn, there were a number of unusual "horse noises" and sounds. Then the horses were led around to the front of the barn and put into their stalls for the night.

The men and I went into the house for supper and at last I got a chance to talk to my dad. He told me in his way the story of the birds and the bees. Now my dad's rendition of the birds and the bees was told in a very unusual manner. He took me over to the brooder house which was nice and clean and had a couple of nice new straw bales to sit on, one for him and one for me.

Now to digress from this story for a few moments, the reader is advised of one important factor: I very much wished, with all my heart, that I could have a baby brother. You see, I was the only child in the neighborhood who had no siblings. I was very much aware of this and constantly kept my parents aware of my wishes. I had no idea what this might entail, only that I wished for a little brother and was completely innocent of anything that needed to happen to get a baby brother.

My father used the following story out in the brooder house that evening, one he felt was very good. Without saying too much, he likened the reproductive process as not unlike gardening, as having seeds that were planted in the mother and developed after planting. So it was that I, as a young child, was thinking, *If seeds from the garden were available to our female horse to have a foal, apparently they could also be available to my mother to have a baby brother.*

To my mother's embarrassment, as well as to everyone else's present at our supper table that evening, I asked Mr. Button to give my mother a seed for a little brother. The room exploded in laughter, and I was confused and embarrassed as that seemed the most applicable solution to me. It was a number of years before I figured that one out!

I suppose that to my way of thinking it was no different than asking for a piece of candy or taking a medication or a pill. Of course, one would have to know how anxious I was for a little brother at that innocent age of four years. It was a surprise to all at the table that evening since it was so subtle and innocent. Of course, I had no idea what caused the explosion of laughter because I thought that my request was perfectly logical, and that very likely that Mr. Button had more than one seed along.

I can remember this event with its rather inconclusive manner of transferring seeds and the laughter that had accompanied my request. I know that my Grandpa Gord was present that evening and he'd had a good laugh and had commented to his daughter, my mother, which also caused additional laughter. That did not surprise me so much because he was always teasing me when I was to wash up for meals by advising, "Be careful. Don't wet the nose."

Gordon at "that innocent age"

*Their horse pulling Gordon and Auntie Helen, with Spot looking on.
This is not to be confused with the "Big Horse."*

Gordon and Spot

Dogs

Well, I have written about most everything else so I might just as well tell about the dogs in my life! I don't remember them all, but when I think how important they were to me, how could I not write about them?

The first dog I remember was one that my Grandpa Henry gave us when he moved off the farm he had homesteaded. The main thing I remember about that dog, Ike, was that he did not like this three -year-old kid, me! Try as I might, I just could not make friends with that brownish-black little border collie. That made me all the more determined to make friends with him—he let me pet him, but he was the only dog I had this experience with. If I got closer than ten feet away from Ike, he was up and moving on away from me. That was something that really bothered me! Apparently, it also bothered the dog, too!

After Ike died we had a couple of non-descript dogs. Then, I had gotten seriously ill and our neighbor, Mr. George J. Reuss, gave me a gift. It was a black and white English shepherd that was perhaps the most loyal, intelligent and faithful dog that I ever did have. I named him Spot. Spot rode on the teeter-totter with me, allowed me to make a harness for him, and pulled a dogsled for me. He was an excellent coon hunter and did a good job of treeing raccoons; he was also an excellent cattle dog and was very good at herding cattle. He was good at hunting ducks and pheasants and did a good job of retrieving them. When I went to country school, he would watch for me to return and when I came into sight a half mile away, he would come and meet me and accompany me home! He was also my guardian and would allow neither man nor beast ever to get close to me, not even my dad!

Then there was a ¾-blood female Airedale that we called Patsy. She was a most excellent and unforgettable dog that reminded me very much of Spot. She was an outstanding hunter of raccoon as well as waterfowl and pheasants! We also enjoyed her little puppies, which we gave away. One of her puppies was remembered by the family we gave it to for staying with a young child who was lost in a grain field. The dog stayed by the child and persistently barked so that the parents could find both the dog and the child. The parents were very grateful! Patsy was very helpful—when it came time to put the laying hens inside in the fall of the year, she could be depended on to catch the hens and hold them down without biting or hurting them.

After I married and raised a family, there was a span of 20 years or so when we raised Spitz puppies. While they are supposed to be house dogs, we found them alerting us when strangers came on the place! They were better than a doorbell! Our children loved to play with the puppies and gave them a good start in appreciating people. They were also good at keeping mice, rats and gophers in check, as well as raccoons and skunks! Their fur had the unusual ability to repel the odor of their interactions with a skunk.

Pet raccoon with Patsy, the Airedale

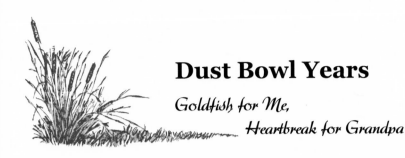

Dust Bowl Years

Goldfish for Me,
Heartbreak for Grandpa

I remember the drought years of the early 1930s and the dust storms that were a part of them. We lived on a mixed farm, raising both livestock and crops. My father would quit fieldwork on days when the wind blew so hard that one could not see! It blew so hard that one can best describe it as similar to a snowstorm or blizzard, only the material blown was dirt and not snow. The consequences of the dust storm were that small grain plants had their roots bared and the plants died. There was no food for either livestock or mankind.

One day we were invited to go and spend an overnight at Grandpa Gord's and Auntie Helen's home. The wind had been blowing somewhat all night so that a slight haze was in the air. You didn't really know in the morning if the wind was going to pick up and get stronger or if you would be able to drive when the visibility became a problem.

We debated back and forth whether to go or not, but there was a special incentive: Grandpa and Auntie Helen were going into Elbow Lake to pick up goldfish at the Drug Store. They were selling a small aquarium with two fish—one gold with a fantail and the other with calico design patches—for a quarter. The fish were very pretty! This was considered a real bargain and had been promoted for some time. In those days of drought and "hard times," this was something the public had been willing to save their pennies for.

The small aquarium was not any bigger than a foot long in all dimensions. It had some fine sand, a small amount of water, and a small sprig of water plant anchored at the bottom. This was considered a great gift in those days of hard earned money!

Grandpa and Auntie had left for Elbow Lake in the wee hours of morning not to miss out on getting the two goldfish and fish bowl. Apparently, they thought there would be a line of people waiting. My mother and I had decided to go up to Grandpa Gord's place, which was about ten miles away, in this dust storm. As the four-year-old grandson, I was to be the recipient of the goldfish. After we got to Grandpa's, we waited for about an hour until they returned from Elbow Lake. The dust storm was severe. We were anticipating unwrapping the goldfish in their habitat and then to "oh" and "ah" over their beauty. The fish lived a fairly long time and I spent many happy hours with my goldfish. The calico one outlived the fantail by a couple of months.

The drought continued and we were so dry that a person could hardly even spit. There was usually something going on at the farm. Grandpa Gord and Auntie Helen had moved in with us. Sounds like fun except that the reason was not fun—it was heartbreaking! They had lost their farm and had to vacate the premises.

It happened like this. Drought conditions seemed to prevail. Grandpa had worked up some low spots of land where there was moisture, seeded them, then hoped and prayed for rain. Believe it or not, it paid off. He got a good crop where he usually hadn't before even in a good year. It was good enough that he could make his final payment on his farm mortgage. The family was rejoicing and with great ceremony the final check was drafted and sent to the F. E. Murphy Loan Co. at Breckenridge. With tears in their eyes, so happy, the check was put in the mailbox. After all that hard work and sacrifice, they now would own the farm.

Unbeknownst to the Henry Gord family, the Grant County State Bank of Herman "threw in the towel" and chose to file bankruptcy on that very day. Grandpa's check for the final mortgage payment—being in transit—was not honored; the Mortgage Company foreclosed and Grandpa lost the farm.

I had heard the story from the family many times as a child, but had the opportunity as an adult to hear about it quite by chance many years later. I had been invited to a Sunday dinner where my friends father-in-law from Wheaton was also invited. He and I got into a discussion of the drought years of the 1930s just by chance. I vaguely mentioned my grandfather's misfortune, and my friend's father-in-law jumped right in wondering if I had heard this story from anyone other than my own family. Upon my saying no, I had not, he urged me to go into Herman in the First National Bank and talk to the president, Mr. Jerome E. Peck. He was quite sure that Mr. Peck would give me a most detailed account of the event that had taken place so many years before.

I followed up on the suggestion and got a full running account of the day that the Grant County State Bank "threw in the towel." At the time, there were two banks in Herman—the one in question and the First National Bank of Herman. I talked to Mr. Peck, who recalled the day of the bank closing. Jerome Peck, now the owner, had been a young man in the 1930s working in the First National under his father at that time.

He told the story like this: On the day in question, the CEO and President of the Grant County State Bank, Mr. Wells, had paid a courtesy call in the morning to Jerome's father, Earnest E. Peck, the President and CEO of the First National Bank of Herman. Mr. Wells wanted to apprise Mr. Peck of the fact that by consent of the board of the Grant County State Bank, it would be closing that very evening at the close of the business day and would not open again. Mr. Wells thought that the First National should follow suit. Jerome Peck said his dad, Ernest E. Peck, told Mr. Wells to get out and that the First National would be staying open until they were as broke as those who banked with them. That never happened and First National continued for many years thereafter!

Walter Ekberg's large herd of cattle (1930)
He was one of the first in the area to raise feeder cattle.

Cattle Feeding

And a House of Straw

Our cattle feeding enterprise was a good one! My dad shared with me some of the events even at the young age of four years. Well, it was like Topsy, it just grew! I am not sure what came first, I'd guess a need for more money.

First off, Dad had a few choice feeder cattle. My grandfather, Frank A. Ekberg, together with friend and neighbor, Victor Hanson, and Dr. Philip Jordon, superintendent of the West Central Experiment Station at Morris, enjoyed a mutual companionship because all three were Purebred Registered Beef Shorthorn breeders. All three had access to herds of fine cattle! Dr. Jordon managed the fine herd of the West Central Station, while Hanson and Ekberg had herds of their own.

Whenever a beef shorthorn event was scheduled, the three would pool rides. They enjoyed being called the "Big Three" of the Shorthorn Breeders of Minnesota. My father, Walter C. Ekberg, selected his first offering of some good quality animals from my grandfather's stock to be fed out to put on the market. Dad's first group numbered 25 or 30 animals that had been raised on our farm. Dad needed the money and fed them up. They looked very nice and he did make some money! We were in business, but we lacked housing and equipment.

The local pharmacist had an old Auburn car, which my father bought and turned into a grain truck; it also had a stock rack that could be put on when hauling cattle. In later years we made the running gear into a hay rack—we still have the running gear to this day!

My dad did a lot of careful planning, which became evident when he started to work on a pit silo to store silage for the cattle. It was located right near our road and ran from our driveway at the north end and went right straight south out into the marsh (then dry because of the drought). The pit was about 30 feet wide and about a150 feet long and about seven feet deep. We started doing the excavating with a team of horses and a scraper, and then graduated to a two-wheeled scraper and a model "D" John Deere that had "lugs" on its steel wheels and worked really well. We would start to fill it up by the north end and go straight south, filling the scraper until it was full. We then flipped a lever that would cause the scraper to come out of the ground, riding on the two wheels, which would go out into the marsh basin and be dumped out there. It took us about two weeks to complete the pit to my father's satisfaction.

Next came the manufacturing of a silage carrier cable, the cable that would carry the wooden cart filled with silage for the cattle down the hill. This cable was attached to a thick, heavy pole at the north end of the pit and down to the other heavy pole at the far end out in the marsh. The cable itself was a work of "art" constructed by my father and his helper. It happened that a telephone wire was to be taken down, so Dad asked to buy it because it would cost so much more to buy it at a store in town.

My dad had his thinking cap on during the formation of the feedlot and the conveyance system for the silage, and many people came to see it. How he made the cable was not the least of his ingenious plan! To make the cable, he first brought the telephone wires home, then strung seven of these smooth telephone wires between the two poles at each end of the silo pit. Next he secured two big grain drill wheels on the north end, where he then strung the seven wires through the seven holes in the 1/8th inch thick steel plate. Once anchored, he could turn the drill wheel manually using leather gloves. We took great care to do a smooth job of twisting the seven telephone wires into one strong cable. It took us about a week to make an excellent, cost-efficient cable to hold the silage carrier. The four-foot by six-foot by three-foot silage carrier was like a wooden box with a trap door on the bottom. When released, the silage dropped into strategically located feed bunks. The silage carrier went down the cable in zip-line fashion several times a day. We no longer had to carry silage from the silo pit to the bunks!

The next part of my dad's feedlot plan was making the cost-efficient straw shed shelter for the cattle. It was made by using hog wire to make the "walls," which were actually three-feet-wide alleys filled with insulating flax straw. The shed was about 40 feet by 60 feet and 10 feet high. The roof was also formed from the wire and flax straw. There was room for 50 head of cattle in this shelter when needed. The hay feeder south of this straw shed pretty much completed the cattle-feeding enterprise, except for a brooder house in which we stored ground ear corn and soybean oil meal. These last two products were spread on top of the silage to add extra protein when fed to the cattle.

Dad next proposed to acquire cattle to feed. He would go to farm auction sales and bid on the cattle, of which there were generally some on each farm auction. We would go to the sale early in the day and look at cattle. My father would size up the cattle for weight—he generally could guess the weight within ten pounds. He kept a record and weighed every animal that we bought so he knew exactly how we were coming out financially. He generally had competition at the auction, and had figured out how much he could afford. If the price was going too high, he quit bidding!

When we first started to feed cattle in the 1930s, the ration was ground whole ear corn on top of silage. At first, we top-dressed that with raw linseed oil meal. Then in the late 1930s, soybean oil meal was added for the protein supplement and hay was available for feed.

At the recommendation of the extension service, we fed oyster shells—it was thought that oyster shells stimulated the cattle's stomachs for more efficient gains and more profitability! When the cattle were fat enough and ready to market, they were taken off alfalfa hay and given a good prairie hay so they would not have loose stomachs when they were shipped to the stockyards. The protein was cut for the same reason!

Because Dad was very thorough in his feeding and marketing, he had a good reputation in South St. Paul. He used the same commission company all the time—the Minnesota Livestock Commission run by the Lenerety Brothers, Joseph and George, with Mabel Riley in charge of the office. Dad always went along with the trucker when he sold cattle, and the buyers knew Dad and that he had done a good job of feeding. He even saw to it that the pens had fresh straw and spent time currying with the comb and brush so that the cattle looked good and saleable.

Dad was one of the first large cattle feeders in Minnesota, reaching up to some over 200 head. Cattle were branded to go to Park Rapids, Minnesota, in the drought years. Then the rains came and we didn't have to go! Looking back on the cattle feeding enterprise, I can see where we had done a most excellent job all the way!

Gordon's herd of dark red Angus

Gordon (lower left) at the sales barn near Sisseton, SD, for sale of his first Angus herd. This was a heartbreaking day for Gordon, to have to sell the herd he had developed. We surmise it was not feasible to maintain his herd financially at that time due to feed prices, pasture land, etc.

Horses

If I said I was going to write about the early days of farming in Minnesota and did not include horses, there would not be much to tell! Why? Because horses were the power plant that gave the energy to Minnesota agriculture in the days before mechanization. Oh, if we wanted to give credit for all units of energy, we would have to include oxen and mules, but they would have represented a very limited source of energy. Using any source of energy other than horses was or could be attributed to personal preference; sometimes farmers had already built an energy source, or a parent or relatives had given a new farmer either oxen or mules from their surplus. Now don't get me wrong—there are good points from all three! I know that if I had been a young farmer back in those days and someone offered to "gift" me either oxen or mules, I certainly would not have been apt to turn anything down. I would not have "looked a gift" mule or oxen in the mouth!

Now laying those arguments aside, the new young farmer generally started with a team of horses, which for all practical purposes is two horses, and then added one as resources and finances allowed. The usual team was a mare (female) and a gelding (a neutered male). The young owner of a mare would often have her bred by a stallion (male), after paying a breeding fee to the owner of the stallion. This was often done. The aim was to increase the horse herd to a minimum of four horses, so that a machine of standard size could be pulled by a four-horse team. A drill that would place the grain evenly is a machine that required four horses. Other machines that required four horses included a sulky plow to turn the ground over, a disc to pulverize lumpy ground, a digger and a four- or five-section drag, which would nicely prepare the ground for the grain drill. Those were generally the most popular machines requiring four horses.

We had stalls for eight horses when I was a boy of five or six. Actually, our barn had stalls for 16 horses, but we made half of the stalls into calf pens when we cut down the number of horses we had on hand. In the early days my grandfather had been a horse trader who bought and sold horses, thus the barn had been built for having more horses on hand for the horse trading business. His children, my father and uncles, used to get so disgusted—once they got the horses well-trained so that they drove well and responded to them, then the horses became all the more attractive to "horse traders." So, they were always hoping to see the horse trading business fade out.

The story is told of when Grandfather acquired a "balky" horse that did not respond to commands and when the dog came near, the horse would not move or go ahead. Grandfather, who after trying for some time, thought that he would teach the horse a good lesson. Grandfather took some dry hay and built a fire under the horse and then commanded the animal to go ahead. The horse went ahead alright, but only enough that it placed the buggy square over the fire and the buggy caught fire! Needless to say, Grandfather soon got rid of that horse!

During the dry years of the 1930s my dad thought that, since I was now six or seven years old, I should be old enough to herd cows when the pastures were turning brown and drying up—but it was too much for me to look after a fairly large herd of some 30 cows. What I needed was a riding pony so I could cut off the cattle when they made the effort to get to the next clump of green grass. So my dad borrowed the neighbor boy's pony. The neighbor boy, Rudy Raths, was about four years older than me. He had a quarter horse named "Star," which he gladly loaned to us for the herding season.

That gave me the idea to get a pony, too! So, the next year when my dad went out to the Dakotas buying feeder cattle, he picked up a good well-trained pony for me! That was how I got Polly, who saved my life during the Armistice Day snow storm.

My father also got me a saddle that had an interesting history. It seems the saddle had been confiscated from a rodeo participant. It was a 90-pound saddle that I was unable to lift, so I got some ropes and block and tackle to assist me in saddling my pony. The saddle was nice to ride on but most inconvenient to get the pony saddled, so we did not keep it long.

We had many different horses, but the favorite was Babe, a Western branded bronco. She was always causing runaways, and when Dad had her on the hay mower she only had all four feet on the ground but a couple of times in 20 minutes. Dad bought her with the assurance that she was well broke, but even with her unruliness she was still a good horse. We owned her for over 20 years until she died of old age. It was a sad day for us when we traded horses for tractors, but it was a good financial decision and a necessary one!

We were the first family in the area to have the Allis Chalmers Row Crop tractor and the second family to purchase the Allis Chalmers All-Crop Harvester combine. This combine was purchased from Anton Christianson at Wendell. In 1933, Lewis Derby (my wife's grandfather who passed before her birth) came to the farm to write an article about the combine for the local newspaper.

Grandpa Gord hauling manure

Dairy

I was born into the realm of a Dairy Farm. The milk cows we had when I was a kid were milking shorthorns and some of them would equal the production of a good Holstein. I was about six when I started to milk by hand, a real accomplishment, and I always remember my dad who had a crippled left arm and hand. He thought that sitting down and milking a cow was the most relaxing time of the day; it precipitated a good rest for him and he looked forward to milking time. Dad could milk fast, despite being crippled.

We were one of the first farms to get a milking machine and that was interesting. The first machine that we had was a "Page" portable milking machine that you wheeled out behind the cows. It was an all-vacuum machine, which utilized the "suck and blow" principle; most others had a milk inflation system that massaged the cow's udder. Then a few years later we traded the Page machine in for one made by the Surge Company. A few years after that the DeLaval Company gave us a demonstration of their milking machine, which was the kind we kept for as long as we milked cows.

Having a milking machine precipitated us into enlarging our herd, and then from there to selling whole milk instead of separating the milk and the cream; before that we sold the cream and fed the milk to the hogs. When we started selling the whole milk, the pigs missed their milk, so Dad bought buttermilk real cheap from the local creamery for the hogs and all were happy.

I was always trying to improve our herd of cattle, which were being switched over to Holsteins. This was done by testing the milk through the Dairy Herd Improvement Ass'n., who sent a person to take milk samples from each individual cow once a month. As we upgraded our herd, we selected cows that had the highest butterfat. Most Holstein herds had an average butterfat test of about 3.2%.

We bought a bull from Winterthur Farms of Wilmington, Delaware, owned by the Du Ponts. This bull's mother had a butterfat test of 4.5%, so of course he cost more than the average bull. The theory was that the new bull's daughters would reflect 4.5% butterfat when they came into production. We paid about $1,000 for the bull calf, along with railroad expense of $240 to ship him here from Delaware. Read more about him in the next chapter!

When trying to upgrade our herd, someone alerted us to the herd of Mrs. Elise Nelson and Sons from Lake Benton, so we went down there and bought a few head of cows and heifers from them. What we had heard was certainly true; they were a very high milk-producing herd. The volume of milk was high, but it was somewhat low on butterfat percent. We had one of those cows that, after having a calf, produced 92 pounds of milk per day for three months straight, but its butterfat content was only 2.8%; although that was still a pretty good showing and was the reason we purchased the Winterthur bull.

I stayed in dairying for a number of years and then sold out. One of the major reasons was that when my dad went out buying feeder cattle in the fall it also caused an outbreak of shipping fever, which spread from the feeder cattle to the dairy herd. We felt we were on the road to really improving our herd, but another thing changed the outcome of our dairy business. I doctored the dairy cattle after they became sick when we brought in new cattle for the beef-feeding herd. I had such good success that the neighbors noticed and asked me to help them with their sick cattle. This was during World War II, and there was indeed a labor shortage out here in the rural areas—it was hard to get a vet right away when one was needed.

I asked advice from two very good veterinarians from our area who mentored me, Dr. Leslie Stock of Kensington and Dr. John Bush of Chokio. Both were glad to have the help and that was how I came to be asked to be a kind of vet. Appearing to have a good percent of cures, my vet-helping grew. And I liked that—I liked cattle and liked people, and really enjoyed the fact that my subjects responded favorably to my ministrations. It was also a time of good fellowship when I came to treat the sick cattle. Some of the families even baked special coffee cake and had tea for me after I had treated their sick animals. I received many commendations, and to an 18-year-old young man that was quite flattering indeed.

I had joined the Independent Order of Odd Fellows (IOOF), which I really enjoyed and nearly always asked those whom I was helping to join too. I realized after a few years that my membership had helped the Order grow. My awareness happened like this: in the coat room at lodge a friend who I had done vet work for, pointed out that a person whom I had asked to join several times with no success had apparently become a member—we could see him in the main room through the coat room door. My friend said our mutual friend had told him that he was joining because he likely would have need of my vet services and that I may refuse him if he did not join. He did not want to take the chance that I might not come for a vet call. However, he believed I would not refuse to come if a member called, so he had therefore signed up "just in case." I was so surprised and got a smile out of that kind of thinking, because I would never refuse anyone needing help! Anyway, I had unintentionally gotten into the vet business because of my enjoyment of helping people and because of the natural joy I had working with and doctoring animals.

Looking back, one of the most interesting examples of a serious case of vet work involved a cow with milk fever. Milk fever is lack of calcium in a high-producing dairy cow that has delivered a calf. Perhaps I should define it as an improper loss of fat right after a cow has calved. It usually occurs in a cow sometime after the second or third calf and to a cow that is in good physical condition. It seldom, if ever, happens to a heifer or first-calf cow.

The case that comes to mind when I think of worst case scenarios was an older cow that belonged to Alvin Hedstrom who lived southwest across the field from me. It happened on a Sunday morning with a full-scale blizzard in progress. Of the cases I treated, and I had treated many through the years, possibly 70% were from milk fever. The minute I found out the age of the cow and that she had calved during the night and the calf had sucked the udder a quarter dry and now the cow could not get up, I suspected milk fever, a fairly easy malady to treat. Unfortunately, I'd treated many cows the past week and was all out of the prescribed medication. Because of the blizzard, our road was plugged, so Alvin sent his older son Leland across the field with the tractor.

Well, I did not even want to go over without replenishing my milk fever medicine, so with Leland ready to take me with the tractor I first called the drugstore and apprised the druggist, Mr. Hanson, of my dilemma. Yes, he had an ample supply of milk fever medication on hand at the store. This was a 500cc bottle of calcium, administered intravenously. I asked Mr. Hanson if the snowplow had gone that morning, and it had. Then I asked if it was alright to send Alvin (whom I could notify by phone) to come and get a couple of bottles, one for this case and one to keep on hand.

"Yes," said Mr. Hanson, "send him in."

So I called and explained the situation to Alvin, who willingly obliged and left for town to get the calcium treatment. Leland and I set off across the field to the Hedstrom farm, arriving just as Alvin came back with the calcium from town.

Well, I thought, *We'll soon have the cow up on her feet and on her way to recovery.* We all met in the barn at the same time, but to our dismay it appeared the cow had died because of the delay in getting the medication during the storm. I jumped into the pen and tried to feel a pulse. I thought I would try to raise her blood vein manually, but had no success. I tied a rope about her neck and tightened it in an effort to raise the vein—still no success. It was no small task to get the IV needle in without raising the vein first.

With only one option left, I took the large needle in my right hand and after scrutinizing the animal very carefully I aimed carefully at the location typically used for this procedure and plunged the needle in.

"Any blood coming out of the needle?" Alvin asked. If there was bleeding that would indicate that the needle had entered the vein.

"Yes," I said. There were just a couple of drops of blood coming out the needle, so I quickly attached the I.V. hose to the needle and it started. The medication seemed to go in easily, which would mean that I had miraculously hit the limp vein. A few seconds later the supposedly dead cow took a breath. Then a few seconds later the cow's eyes, which were open but with dust and chaff in them, started to water. Next the cow's tail twitched.

I said to Alvin, "She might make it."

The I.V. bottle was about half empty as the other signs of life appeared. By the time the bottle was completely empty, there was no doubt that she would live and I said a prayer thanking God for a miracle. The Hedstroms were just as thrilled as I was. But that was the most serious case of milk fever I ever treated. The delay because of the storm really caused problems. It was really miraculous that I hit the limp vein and got the medication in!

Just as I unintentionally got into the vet busines, the same thing was true of how I started helping the telephone company. They had trouble getting help on their rural lines when young men were drafted into military service because of the war, so I was often solicited to help. Since I was too young to have a driver's license, I could take the jobs because an older neighbor who was on the telephone board would drive me around. Fixing lines and climbing poles with lineman's climbing spurs was kind of a "heady" thing for a kid who was too young to drive, and I enjoyed that, too. It was not quite as much fun as it could have been, though, because I had to work outside in the cold and snow most every time there was a problem.

Gordon up at 4:30 a.m. to milk cows. He worked hard on the farm to make up for not completing high school, always wanting to prove himself and make his parents proud.

A prize registered Holstein purchased from Mrs. Elise Nelson and Sons of Lake Benton. It produced 93 pounds of milk per day for three straight months.

The Winterthur Bull

I have always had a soft spot in my heart for animals, so it was no surprise that I wanted to milk cows by hand at a very early age and as soon as practical. My dad gave me certain responsibilities for the dairy operation and I was quite pleased. This included raising the dairy calves, which involved teaching a calf to drink milk out of a calf milk bucket. That was not too hard of a job, fun and somewhat messy getting milk spilled on a person, but also rewarding.

In my story about dairying, you will note that I got my cows from a number of different sources. You will also recall that I got my herd's sire bull, or at least one of them, from a special dairy farm out in Wilmington, Delaware. Why did I do this? Because I wanted to improve my herd. How would I improve my herd by buying this bull? Would it enhance my herd by being a beautiful animal? No, that is not what we anticipated. It was for the improvement of the milk test from his offspring daughters, that they would produce higher butterfat that would garner a higher price for the milk, and thus we would profit.

So, the search was on by looking in the *Holstein-Friesians World* magazine because the Holstein breed was attracting a lot of attention. The Holstein is a rather large black and white animal with an average milk test of 3.2% butterfat. The average test of the Winterthur was some over 4.0% that was genetically proven.

The bull grew and developed into a very fine animal. His official name was Winterthur Alert Forbes Flint. He did have a rather irritable disposition and so we had to be mindful of where he was at all times and never let him get behind us, ever. One time, despite our precautions and unknownst to us, he got behind me and tossed his head at me—one of his horns was over a foot long and two inches in diameter! Instead of going into my body, the horn grazed a 12-inch diameter wooden post and gouged a one-inch-deep gash in the post!

My father said, "That is it! We are having his horns cut off by the local veterinarian."

Dr. W. L. Smedley said if the bull's horn had grazed my head instead of the post, I would have been dead! It took protracted effort to secure the animal with heavy rope in a sturdy cattle chute. At one time the bull cornered me in the end of the chute and charged at me head-on before we could secure him! The only way I could save myself was to leap frantically into the air, spreading my legs so the bull went headfirst right between my legs. With a loud crashing sound, he hit the back end of the chute and broke a two-inch thick hardwood plank. What a time we had to secure the animal and then give him a tranquilizer so no one got hurt! After the tranquilizer was administered, the veterinarian sawed the horns off. The bull healed nicely, but I'll never forget that day!

Gordon with his registered Holstein bull, Winterthur, costing $1,000

Pearl Harbor

I remember the day that Japan bombed Pearl Harbor. I had overslept and my mother called upstairs that Pearl Harbor had been bombed. It seemed unreal, but somehow reality gripped the entire nation and there was an all out effort to mobilize. The battle fleet of the U.S. Navy was essentially sunk on December 7, 1941. However, the aircraft carriers were not in Pearl Harbor at the time, so they and other ships were not affected.

Neil Blume with the pelts from the winter he trapped with Gordon

Hunting & Trapping
Waterfowl and Muskrats, Pheasants, Turkeys and Prairie Chickens

I should write something of the topography of our farm and also tell about the "olden days" and present days of hunting on our farm. We have excellent hunting of ducks, geese, deer, and pheasants. We have first-class overnight facilities for hunters and others, and we do have the game and most excellent habitat—in fact, the best habitat for pursuing game. There is a 21-acre pond right next to our building site (we own seven acres of it), and there are well over a dozen ponds/marshes within five miles of our farm site.

There are freshwater shrimp in some of the marshes, and lots of pheasants as well as deer and waterfowl. My dad and his siblings (who were born in the late 1800s) had a regular field day of waterfowl hunting. There were many, many prairie chickens back then—pheasants were not introduced to the area until the early 1930s.

I was a small kid way back in the early 1930s, but I remember when the first Chinese Ringneck Pheasants were released into the wild along a portion of the hillside of Burr Lake. The hillside for over a half mile of Burr Lake's west area was heavily populated with just oodles and oodles of wild chokecherry and wild plum thickets, affording some excellent protection from varmints and the weather. Not to be forgotten or ignored was the generally-scattered manure from the dairy farmers—in the scattered manure were numerous halfway-digested corn and grain kernels from the dairy farms. I know because I often sat in the laps of the hired men who drove the manure spreader that was powered by a team of two horses. This was a by-now-nearly-forgotten supplemental feeding establishment of the Chinese Ringneck in this part of Minnesota. Three times each week when it was time for the farmers to spread manure there was a mass exodus of the newly-released pheasants from the cattails and bulrushes of local marshes where they had taken cover from the varmints and the weather. No wonder they got a good start when first planted here.

Every year the wild resident waterfowl of the area made a big effort to reproduce themselves—ducks and geese were nesting, as were the prairie chickens. According to *A Blossom on the Prairie* by local author, Gary Hedstrom, who did a fabulous job writing about the pioneer days, in 1884 the *Minneapolis Tribune* reported that in this part of Minnesota there was a great multitude of wild waterfowl and prairie chickens hatched that spring. As a result, the hunters, or "nimrods" as they were called, harvested thousands of pounds of geese, ducks and brant as well as upland game birds and shipped them from Herman that fall. Our area has always had a most respectable tally of successful hunting camps.

There were also numerous domestic flocks such as turkeys that were included in the most abundant harvest of fowl. Many families maintained a domestic flock of Bronze Turkeys and sold these along with the wild harvest. We had a small flock, which we dressed and shipped to the Cities. There was real good train/rail service for those shipping fowl to the Twin Cities of Minneapolis/St. Paul, and even further to Chicago. The carcasses were shipped in a light barrel that had plenty of ventilation. The birds were shipped after having been plucked of their feathers and eviscerated by having the innards extracted in a very clever manner. A button hook was inserted in the "vent" and twisted around to encounter the viscera, making it easy to carefully extract the intestines, etc. The carcasses were also carefully laid on a bed of fresh, dry prairie hay and were in very fine shape upon their arrival at their destinations whether that would have been either the Twin Cities or Chicago.

Another thing I have taken note of concerns the flyways used by the ducks, as told to me by my father. The pond right in front of our building site was quite sharply slanted—an incline of about 20 to 40 feet.

The pond really had that striking topography. The pond had an inlet on the northwest and an outlet on the southeast. What my farther marveled at was the flyway primarily from the southeast. After feeding their fill on the abundant freshwater shrimp, the lesser scaup (for which that body of water was famous) took off from the center of the pond. They flew northeasterly, rising above the north shore (which had the highest banks) and flew directly for Burr Lake. That gave hunters two excellent hunting areas: one which they entered from the southeast, and the other when they left from the middle and went directly to the prominent point on Burr Lake.

However, while I was still a small boy, the ducks seemingly changed their flyway and almost always exited in the northwest. Only once did I ever know the ducks to use the flyway that my father had talked about. The lake had been dry for a few years and that may have made the difference. One year, a dry one in the Dakotas, 27 pairs of canvasback nested in that pond, but only that one year. When normal rainfall again was present, the flyway returned to normal with about three pairs of ducks nesting in the pond.

I would like to elaborate on the marsh/pond right south of our farm site. My father had told me a great deal about this body of water ever since I was a child. First of all, my father used it as his main area for trapping muskrats. My dad said he had more than once been rewarded by getting over 400 muskrats in that pond alone.

As far as vegetation goes, the marsh was loaded with cattails and bulrushes, with different types of bulrushes far outnumbering the different types of cattails in the marsh. At the time of my father's trapping, there was far greater water vegetation than there is now—a lot more than I had ever had the privilege of seeing. Much of that was gone when I was a young boy listening to my father's portrayal of the marsh, which he said was one solid stand of the most prolific water vegetation. The muskrats used the roots of the submerged part of the reeds for food, and the rest of the reeds for building material for the many, many houses my dad described.

Dad portrayed the lodging houses and the somewhat smaller feeder houses as most numerous. He had a sled he had built with sides and an end on the back to make it at least two feet higher than normal. The pond had been deeper, but was now about three-and-one-half feet deep as a result of having been exposed to dust storms and the like. Many years later when we had a contractor in to make the islands, the various cutaways and core samples had shown that at one time it could have been up to four feet deeper than the present depth.

The map below will give you an idea of the number of sloughs and ponds in our home township of Macsville.

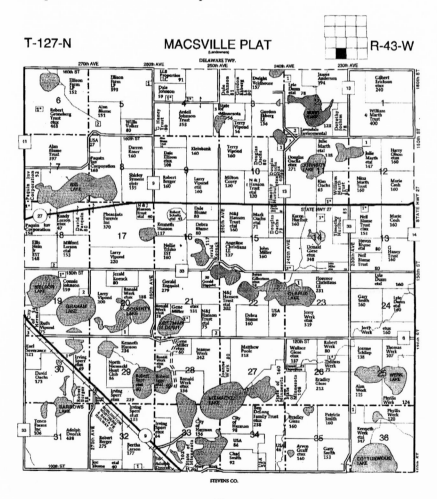

The Odd Fellows

No, No, Not Queer Fellows, But Odd Fellows, For Goodness Sake!

This exclamatory remark is by far more accurate picture of the organization than the word "odd," which while it indicates a deviation from the usual or expected, it fails to present the usual as being some degree of kindness or goodness that is the result of the efforts of the person being recognized as an Odd Fellow!!!

For 68 years I have been a member of the Odd Fellows, or more explicitly, the "Independent Order of Odd Fellows" (IOOF). They give a command in the obligation: to visit the sick, relieve the distressed, to bury the dead, and to educate the orphan.

It happened that I met the Sovereign Grand Master of the Odd Fellows who had flown into Mankato for a meeting and then the next day I was to drive him in my car to Virginia. He was a very fine and wealthy man. He had excellent decorum and conducted the most interesting meetings! Anyway, the next day when we were driving along getting better acquainted with each other he suddenly asked me, "You know the Lord, don't you, Brother Ekberg?"

I said, "Yes, and from the experiences I have had, I would like to deepen my faith." We talked on and on and he suggested that I become a Lay Leader in the church of my choice. The man's name was Oakford Schalick, Sr., and he was from Elmer, New Jersey. He was a well-to-do feed manufacturer and certainly an interesting fellow. It was on his recommendation that I checked out the Methodist Church and applied for instruction and have really enjoyed my years of teaching the Gospel.

I thought about the title of this chapter for a long time, because I have really appreciated and enjoyed the organization and it has had a most prominent place in my life! I know I had noted on many occasions when reading a most interesting book that the author could have told about some interesting and benevolent aspect of the Odd Fellows. We Odd Fellows were the first organization—whether religious, governmental or fraternal—to establish homes for our elderly members, as well as for the orphan children of our members. The author could have taken the opportunity to lead into a very interesting article, but no, instead wrote only of the ordinary and mundane.

I decided that if I ever had the opportunity to really express my great admiration for the Odd Fellow organization, I would do so! It is the friendliest, kindest, most caring organization I know of!

Does our concern for the elderly and orphans sound like being kind? The dictionary defines "kind" as being of a friendly, generous or warm-hearted nature, as well as having a charitable and understanding nature. Does that sound like a good or nice person to know or to be? With those commands being paramount in our hearts and minds this does seem to be a good and desirable organization to belong to, doesn't it?

An outstanding example of the Odd Fellows' concerns for their fellow man has to be the fact that the Odd Fellows were the very first group to establish a home for their aged in Meadville, Pennsylvania. Following the establishment of the home for the aged, there was the home for the orphans, that provided as well for their education!

The Odd Fellow-sponsored Pilgrimage for Youth was just such a program, with its historic tour of the New York City/Washington, D.C. area, providing significant opportunities to enrich youthful minds and efforts. The Odd Fellows care for their fellow man and do things to let them know it. It is a fraternal social organization—that is to say they show and demonstrate comradery. I had heard it said in this manner, but never really understood the explanation. For fraternity—unless embedded in acts of humanity—is but an empty name. To visit the sick and the lonely is but an empty phrase. To relieve the distressed (by that I mean someone I can talk to and express my innermost feelings and not be "made fun of"). To be there when one feels "down and out."

I value the attributes of Oddfellowship more as the years go by! When I know that a person believes in and subscribes to the teaching of Oddfellowship, I know they are really special. When one thinks of Odd Fellows, one thinks automatically of Good for Life and kindness.

Some of the programs that Odd Fellows subscribe to are really proof of what they think and do:

- The homes for the aged;
- The orphanages and Children's Villages for homeless youth;
- The scholarship programs to enhance education in most jurisdictions.

The many and varied programs are evidence that we care.

The fact that one of our own in our little village of Herman, Dr. A. D. Larson, M.D., did indeed become a state jurisdictional legislator and helped pass a bill into law years ago that required "gasoline cans be painted red, thus alerting the public of the danger." This has saved many lives.

The Odd Fellows and Rebekahs Visual Research Foundation is another area of human kindness to our fellow man. For example, the Wilmer Eye Institute of the Johns Hopkins Hospital of Baltimore, Maryland, has been at the forefront of eye research and patient eye care since it was founded in 1925. The Odd Fellows and their sister organization, the Rebekahs, teamed up with Wilmer and Johns Hopkins by giving an endowment of 2.5 million dollars. The plan was to increase that endowment to 3 million dollars to our members and friends.

A part of this program includes "Big Eye Magnifier Lamp" programs. The magnifier lamps enhance reading ability for many with visual problems who are pursuing hobbies, crafts, fine arts, and any areas of special work. How do these two programs become available to us? Contact the local Odd Fellow or Rebekah Lodge. The Lodge will do it!

In addition to the programs mentioned above, our scholarship opportunities in the Education Foundation help young people prepare for life itself!

We offer:
- Scholarships
- Low rate student loans
- Education opportunities in the Educational Pilgrimage for Youth to New York City and Washington, D.C.

We also participate in the National Arthritis program. And then there are our wonderful lodges where our aim is to lead many to cultivate the true fraternal relationship designed by the Great Author of His Being. After all that, we should take a rest and go on vacation—many of our Jurisdictions do maintain summer recreational resorts, such as the one at Cleveland, Minnesota.

Jewel presentation event at IOOF:
front, l-r: Wally and Marvin Andersen, Gordon
back: Dennis Hedstrom (next to Gordon)

The Light of My Life and a Family

One day I noticed that some of my mother's spoon collection were gone. Now, this was around 50 years ago. I asked her about that and she said that she had given it to one of my cousins to remember her by. I thought that was odd, and then I thought, *Well, I hope there are other mementos of her things left for me to give my wife and family, if I ever get married.* Then I realized that I had never had a serious girlfriend. No wonder she was giving away keepsakes!

I had taken different girls out, but nothing had clicked and here I was in my 40s and still single. Had I never given the subject much thought? Well, no—but that really wasn't true either, because I had definitely considered the subject of marriage ever since the age of nine. I reasoned that I had 11 years before I reached the age of 21, at which time I should be able to get married. Plenty of time! I had so many interesting things to do and the time just went by. Then the thought came to me, *What if everyone thought that I was too old to get married, what then?* It was a concern because I longed for a wife and family, but never let on that this was true.

I decided that the thing to do was to write to the Peace Corps and volunteer! I did want my life to count for something and this I thought was a good thing and it would help people. Well, I did write to the Peace Corps and received a nice letter and an application. But the very next Sunday, Pastor Lloyd Osborn had a heart attack. They could not find anyone to take the services for the next Sunday. Since I had gone to the

District Superintendent in Wadena to be a lay speaker, the Church Board gave me a call to see if I might take over until they got someone, which I accepted. Pastor Osborn was laid up for some time and the Board asked if I might continue for a while through the summer.

I was open to continuing because I simply enjoyed speaking… and then I had noted a most attractive young woman in the congregation. I gathered from whom she was sitting with who her family might be and knew them all, but I had never met the young woman in question. Now, I wanted to find out just who she was. And as a shy individual, I certainly was not going to give any idea to anyone that I was interested.

So, I asked Leonard Blume as casually as I could if that was all the Harvey Derby family sitting there. I asked about others in attendance so that it was simply an inquiry about who my audience had been. Then by careful checking, I found out that Gay Adele Derby was the young woman in question. Now, did I dare find out if she would go out with me?

I had a sample of special oats that I had hired a few young high school boys to hand clean, among whom was Gay's younger brother, Ron. I got well acquainted with him and after a couple months dared to ask him to find out if Gay would go out with me, seeing that I was 20 years older! Boy! Don't think that I didn't pray that she would find me acceptable and go out with me! I could hardly wait to talk to her brother Ron. Was I ever relieved when Ron told me, "Yes!"—she would accept a date with me!

Well, I finally got up the nerve to call up to Aitkin, Minnesota, where Gay was teaching, and I was hoping and praying that her answer would be yes. And it was! I was so careful about calling that I didn't call on my home phone in case her answer would be no. What did I do? I called from a phone booth in Wendell just before Thanksgiving. I decided to ask her to go to a show in Alexandria and to lunch afterwards. Was I ever elated to get an affirmative answer!

I was concerned after the movie, Patton, started as the general language was rather risqué. But when I brought her home, I asked if she would like to go out with me again! I was delighted when she said yes and doubly delighted when she made a nice lunch for our second date—a ski trip to Holloway Hill at Maplewood State Park near Pelican Rapids. After that, we went out every weekend. Gay drove home from Aitkin where she was the school speech therapist, nearly a three-hour drive. We had a number of outings together and really enjoyed each other's company.

Gay's dad and brother teased her that very likely I thought she would make a good member of the Odd Fellow/Rebekah Lodge and that I would be asking her to join that lodge. As far as they knew, I, Gordon Ekberg, was more interested in lodge than marriage. Little did they know! We went together for six months when I finally asked Gay to marry me. She said yes, and in June 1972 we picked out the engagement ring and wedding bands. Six months later, just before Christmas, we were married on December 23. We honeymooned in Daytona Beach, Florida.

Gay went back to teaching in Aitkin and I went back to the farm. We were together almost every weekend, either in Aitkin or Herman. Our next big event was when we learned we were to be parents. Kris Ann Konvally Ekberg was born February 19, 1974. Amy Lee Ekberg was born June 3, 1975.

The next big event was the death of my father-in-law, Harvey W. Derby, in July 1975. He had not been feeling well and died at a young age from cancer. That was most unexpected and sad.

Joel Alan Ekberg was born February 25, 1977. Interestingly, even before we met, we had both decided that if we had a son, his name would be "Joel." We discovered this in a conversation a week after being married. Then our fourth child was a girl whom we named "Vangie", short for Evangeline Grace Ekberg who was born on July 24, 1979. We loved the name "Vangie," which we had discovered at a wedding when a flower girl had the name card by her plate. We decided that if we ever had another child, we hoped it could be a girl and that we would love to name her "Vangie"—and that is what happened!

Then we had a miscarriage and lost a child, and was that ever a traumatic experience! I had never ever dreamt that would affect Gay and me both, seeing that the baby had never lived so that we could become acquainted with it. But that was most definitely the case!

Then after a few years, we discovered that we were going to have a fifth child, and the neighbors were wondering how many are we going to have? John Gordon Ekberg was born on March 19, 1983. Gay and I enjoy our rather large family and appreciate them all!

Gay and I have had a wonderful life together. She has been "one in a million." I had been smart to wait those extra years for the right one to come along. I am constantly amazed at her outstanding ability in most every area! Ours has been that marriage typified by excellent teamwork—I couldn't be happier!

Gay Adele Derby and Gordon Frank Ekberg on wedding day
December 23, 1972

The Art Gallery

*Artist Days, Extra Work and
Prairie Dance Halls*

At one time we had well over 150 waterfowl on hand as prized breeding stock. There were swans, wild geese and wild ducks in the natural habitat pens and equipment to go with it. As a result of the many waterfowl, many visitors came to view the birds in their habitat, and the many beautiful pictures by well-known artists in our gallery.

Did we ever officially plan ahead for the great amount of activity that ensued because of our waterfowl? No, we had no idea of the amount of interest we were generating because of our own personal interest in wildlife. We did, however, enjoy the many visitors and guests and wanted to share with them.

Well, how did this all start? I've told this story so many times, you would think I would get tired of answering that question. The answer is that it all started "quite innocently!" The year was 1933 and we were going to celebrate Thanksgiving by having roast duck for dinner. Sounds good. Sounds pretty simple—however, enter a four-year-old little boy, Gordon F. Ekberg, who was seeing some mallard drakes for the first time in his life. There were four mallard greenhead drakes in full color—no wonder I was so spellbound. They were so beautiful.

I asked, "What are we going to do with them?"

"Eat them," said my father.

"Oh, no! Please don't do that," I pleaded. "They are too pretty to eat..." and on went the dialogue until I had discovered there is such a thing as a mama duck that can lay eggs and hatch baby ducklings. Well,

~ 69 ~

I immediately wanted to see if we could trade a Daddy Duck for a Mama Duck, and we were in the duck raising business. Can you imagine a four-year-old child suggesting we trade the Mama Duck back again? Not at all, not a chance! We are still raising waterfowl.

Well, not like we used to do—that was a lot of work and effort expended by the whole family! Now time marches on, and I had failed to consider just what the aging process might do to all of us! First, to myself as the primary caretaker—gathering and then hatching eggs is an experience that just really inspires a person and I could never, so it seemed, tire of the day-to-day chores. What is that verse that says, "The spirit is indeed willing, but the flesh is weak"? Well, it still didn't really occur to me that I had to slow down.

Second, the children who were the main guides for tours were growing up and going off to college. Third, my wife Gay was teaching school full-time and was always helping whenever needed. On the Artist Days she always made a special meal for the guest artists, taking note of their favorite foods!

Often, we would have a special event such as a seminar or an artist day when we could have easily entertained over 200 people and fed them. And we did enjoy doing this. The artist days and other special events plus our other livestock enterprises took a lot of extra work and really kept us busy!

Regardless of the number of species of waterfowl we were raising, it always seemed there was still room for one more. We used to decorate for special events and that was extra work. On regular weekends, we could generally count on at least 20 or more people. This built kind of gradually—but no, that is not true either. Actually, the weather was the main factor.

When we added another species to our flock, it caused extra work. For instance, we would start having more predator problems because our natural habitat pens were right on the edge of a marsh where skunks, raccoons, mink, foxes and weasels would come in. Without even half trying, we became trappers because we had to protect the birds. And as long as we were trapping up by the buildings, we might as well go a little further afield and make it more worthwhile... and so we were now not only bird-raisers, but trappers as well!

Then we had artists coming to the place because they wanted to use live birds as models for accuracy. Well, then we thought we might as well sell prints done by the artists, and the need arose to frame those prints, so we bought framing equipment. Without even realizing it, we were now a full-fledged art gallery. Were we enjoying all the extra work? Yes, we were.

Then there was a need for knick-knack merchandise. Not everyone wanted a $200-$300 print, so we had to have merchandise for all pocketbooks. And then people spent considerable time enjoying our business and we were out in the country with no restaurant available... so we put in a lunch counter.

So you see, like the character "Topsy" our business kept expanding. We enjoyed it because we loved people. And it didn't stop there, because we put on seminars, and other events such as special Artist Days.

One of the main Artist Days featured Jim Meger. And this was quite interesting because Jim had asked me to look around the country for interesting subjects to paint. And so one day I took time to take pictures—of what, I didn't know—I just started off taking pictures of prairie, crops and landscape. When it got to be afternoon I was over east of our place, down by Don McCollor's. Across the road from his house was a run-down building that looked as if it had been pounded into the ground like an iron stake. I did not know what the building was, but it looked interesting so I snapped a number of pictures, both inside and outside.

I packaged the film and sent it to Jim Meger, not really expecting to hear too much from that day's work. But lo and behold, a couple of days later here comes a phone call from Jim Meger.

"Where in the world did you take those pictures?" Jim Meger's voice challenged over the phone.

"Oh, just around my area," I told Jim. I had identified the pictures by numbers, because a lot of them I did not know what they were.

Jim asked about number 18, and I guessed that I thought it was an old cattle shed, which Jim said was "way off" as he had made the rounds of reference possibilities. He said it was kind of out of its usual domain, typically being farther west in the Dakotas—so said the Minnesota Historical Society!

"Well, what do they call it?" I asked, by now almost ill with curiosity.

"Well, hold onto your hat! They said that their best guess was that it was a "Prairie Dance Hall!" Jim said.

I had never heard of such a thing out here in western Minnesota. When I asked what are its identifying characteristics, Jim said that it is built halfway into the ground to be warm in the winter and cool in the summer and usually had a rather wild reputation.

I said, "That does seem to fit what it looks like, but I can't really believe that is what it is!"

So I called Donald McCollor by phone and bluntly asked if it was a "Prairie Dance Hall."

There was complete silence on the other end of the line. Finally a hoarse voice said, "Yeah, that's what it is."

Apparently there had been a family disagreement between parents about whether or not that should be built on McCollor's property.

At any rate, Jim Meger considered it a major "find" out here and painted a major painting from it. But that is not the end of the story!

Before the scheduled day for release of the "Prairie Dance Hall," a major piece of printing had been done to advertise that Jim Meger was to appear in person. But as the appointed and confirmed hour came and went, no Jim Meger. So, I finally called and discovered that Jim had forgotten the date—and we had a yard and gallery full of people waiting to see him!

Jim was shocked that he had forgotten the date, and told me that each of the families present would receive a free, small version for coming, and that he would be here in a little over two hours. We had those who were present sign a paper so that if they were on a time schedule and had to leave, they would still be assured of a smaller print for free.

At any rate, we enjoyed the artists and our association with them. It was a most memorable time of our lives.

Author and photographer, Bruce Burk (California), visited Lawndale Farm 1983 to include photos of the waterfowl in his series of bird books. Also, well-known artist Terry Redlin visited the farm to tour the waterfowl area.

We also became friends of knick-knack salesmen and others who called on a regular basis. Most generally our days and lives were filled with friendships and friends.

Art gallery opens

Wrapping up the remodeling of the old granary into an art gallery by Mark Oachs (sitting at the new counter) and crew. Visitor legislator Charlie Berg (left) stopped by to check on the progress at Lawndale Farm. Next three in picture are Doug Oachs, Butch Blasing,(work crew members) and Eric Magnuson (who worked part-time at the gallery in sales.)

Vising with the artists: Mario Fernandez, Gordon and Gay, Sharon Wald

Jim Meger adding a remarque to the print "Prairie Dance Hall" at the art gallery

Agriculture and the Environment

Now this is one of the reasons for this book: I have seen so many reasons for being disturbed and I just did not feel that as farmers we were on the right track. Now don't ask me why because I can't give an intelligent answer. It is just a "gut feeling." I have a profound faith in God and I have always felt that He made this earth and this wonderful Creation and we should follow as much as possible His prescription for doing agriculture.

For example, in the Bible God points out that land should be rested after every seven years of being farmed. Now that does not seem an unreasonable stipulation at all to me nor does it to numerous other individuals throughout the globe, this world in which we live and move and have our being.

One of those individuals who tried his best to farm as God proclaimed is a God-fearing, God-loving man from the little town of Farwell, Minnesota. David McIver has used a simple formulation in getting a bumper crop without benefit of crossbreeding plants or animals. He doesn't use fertilizer as we know it, but instead uses *Growers Mineral Solutions* at a fraction of the cost of fertilizers and pesticide sprays. How long has he used this alternative choice? A couple of years? No, he has used this alternative for 40 years or more, and has become absolutely convinced of its economical savings as well as its ability to increase yields. Another beneficial message strongly advanced is to use limestone, or in other words calcium, instead of any type of fertilizer. This is one of the most widely-used, readily available and economical elements on the planet.

BE CONSIDERATE TO THE BEES, "THE CANARY IN THE COAL MINE"

Past Ten Years of Chemical Impact Continues Reducing Bee Colony Size: The Big Picture

By Gay A. Ekberg for the *Herman-Hoffman Tribune*, January 2016

Local beekeeper Steve Ellis is relentless in seeking avenues in which to protect the bees from toxic chemicals and to force society to take a long, hard look at ways to ensure the future of these pollinators, which are vital to food production. In 2015 his colony was reduced by 67%, this versus a loss of 10-15% in a typical year, that typical year being before the widespread use of neonicotinoids in agriculture. To make up for this loss, Steve needs to purchase bees from bee raisers in the southern states.

Steve has a simple mantra: "Think. If it doesn't feel right, dig deeper, ask questions." He wants to inspire people to become assertive, not accepting products that may not be adequately tested before being marketed to the public. He has taken on this struggle against EPA (Environmental Protection Agency) and three chemical companies (Bayer, Syngenta, Monsanto) to see that they are required to conduct adequate testing before releasing products for public use or consumption. For example, take a pink coated kernel of corn; ingesting 3 to 4 seeds will be fatal for the unsuspecting pheasant grazing in the fields. Pheasants Forever is asking for an immediate ban on the treated seeds. Since 2005 people are becoming aware of the decrease in bobolinks and meadowlarks, pheasants, ducks, and bees. 2005, the year the treated seeds were available on the market. "2005- all kinds of things started changing."

He is making progress in waking up big companies into realizing their impact on the lives of the bees and the environment. So far Steve has filed lawsuits against Bayer and Syngenta, which are two of the three neonicotinoid companies. Steve is now part of a consolidation, formed after much effort, of twelve organizations (ex: Pheasants Forever, Natural Resources Defense Council, Sierra Club, Center for Biological Diversity, Center for Food Safety, Xerxes Society, etc.), thus gaining clout. As Steve's father, who is a lawyer, said there is "civilized warfare in the courtroom."

One of the newer groups coming forward with concerns over chemicals is the American Bird Conservancy. They are finding that as chemicals affect invertebrates living in the water, those birds who feed on the invertebrates in the ponds and lakes are having their health and lives threatened. This causes Steve to wonder why he hasn't seen any crawfish in the small lake in front of his home at Barrett.

Along with asking questions and digging deeper, one might also question other practices such as raising genetically altered salmon, which grow at an almost alarming rate, and then are fed to the public. There is no testing for our security, but this process is accepted due to GRAS (generally regarded as safe.) That does sound a bit lame when considering what we may ingest and what may affect our health.

Steve's main concern right now is in reaching the ears of the farmers. He urges farmers to be concerned about the increasing chemical costs, question if there is in fact resulting greater yields, ask why their untreated seed cannot be planted, question why they have no choice but to buy treated seed, and continue to ask questions. Compare today's yields with 2005. He wants to increase awareness of alternatives to using the chemicals which impact bees. For example, he points out that when soybeans and corn were first coated with neonics in 2005, the soybean aphids appeared on the scene the very same year. The reason being that the chemical killed the lacewing, which had beforehand attacked the aphids. A solution could be to reintroduce the lacewing to attack the aphids, which would be one fourth the cost of using more chemicals to kill the aphids. Steve wants to bring information to farmers, ways to save expense of chemicals, and yet also increase yields. It seems someone is taking away from the profits and "they should be upset about that." "Farmers are not being given correct information."

Scientists recently have documented in test plots that it is advantageous to go back to the "natural" state. Entomologist and agri-ecologist Dr. Jonathan Lundgren conducting USDA laboratory research for the U.S. Dept. of Agriculture's Agricultural Research Service at Brookings, South Dakota, is currently in controversy with his employers. Although in 2012 he was given an award for his scientific work, his recent investigations have caused an upset. His research, since classified as a "sensitive" topic, disclosed in his paper that one neonic by Bayer was harming Monarch butterflies in their habitat and food source. The chemicals on fields had invaded the milkweed that the grub feeds on, leaving the little infants foraging on toxic food. He also alluded to chemicals meant to destroy aphids were not as effective for that purpose but were in fact reducing the population of its natural predator (dragonfly) of the aphids. This being a case in which nature would better take care of the situation.

Jonathan Lundgren is now involved in a "whistle blower" lawsuit, has stepped down from his formal position, and needs financial support to continue his efforts in independent research (Blue Dasher Farm Initiative.) He intends to set up a national network of Centers for Excellence in regenerative farming, stating a need for "metamorphosis in food production using nature's principles." The American Honey Producers just sent him $25,000. He is seeking support from farmers, consumer, and beekeepers. Lundgren is pursuing testing in agricultural production and impact on water, wetlands, and waterfowl and will focus on research, education, and demonstration. Learn more at: www.bluedasher.farm.

In the midst of all this: "VICTORY! An important win for bees and our food system." This was written on a large postcard sent out by Earthjustice to supporters. On the flip side it explains: "Federal Court Overturns EPA Approval of Pesticide that is Killing Bees." It happens that Earthjustice working with the beekeeping industry reversed the approval of one pesticide called sulfoxaflor. The victory favors the beekeepers, bees, and our food system. Showing this card to Steve Ellis was no news to him. He sat in the courtroom the day this was presented before three judges in San Francisco in the spring of 2015. Hearing the arguments presented by EPA and DuPont Ellis believed the overwhelming evidence would result in that victory. A victory, but also only one of the steps needed.

January 7th headlines read: "The EPA finally Admitted That the World's Most Popular Pesticide Kills Bees-20 Years Too Late" by Tom Philpott. While now admitting to such dire results, they could "restrict or limit their use" by the end of this year. Another step taken forward.

Can a person wash off your fruits and vegetable and will that be okay? No, says Steve, the chemical can be inside your food. You can't wash it off. Steve laments, "No one ever asked, was it okay to put chemicals into my food." Steve comments this has taught him one thing: to be safe. He wants companies to be responsible for what it presents to the public. He only asks that companies conduct good independent studies with proper testing before putting it out to the public. EPA has hedged on this saying this insecticide is not a pesticide when used as a coating and is therefore excluded from pesticide regulations. In Ellis vs. EPA, Steve expects seeds to be registered with proper testing beforehand for the bees' protection. Steve survived the preliminary challenge and is going to have the case argued before the judge in San Francisco this spring-summer.

Steve added the following specific history, in his words: The two national beekeeping organizations, The American Beekeeping Federation and the American Honey Producers Association responded to this industry-wide threat by forming a Bayer-Beekeeper dialogue committee. David Hackenberg (in 2005, first beekeeper to sound alarm of neonics impact on bees) and Steve Ellis were both appointed by their industry as founding members. At these meetings with Bayer Crop Science, the beekeepers were assured that the kind of mortalities seen in Europe couldn't happen here because the neonicotinoid insecticide was securely adhered to the seed, and would not drift off. Despite these assurances, drift off incidents of bee kills were occurring in the U.S. Steve Ellis reported a number of such bee kills, one which can be viewed on You Tube http://youtu.be/xxXXalLuK5s. The Bayer Bee Dialogue committee found the discussions with Bayer to be fruitless and focused their energies into discussions with the EPA. Through 3 years of intense communication, and face-to-face meetings as representative of the

National Honey Bee Advisory Board, Steve learned that the EPA was not willing to take action to restrict this class of chemicals...travels to Washington, D.C., meeting, conferences, and connections...it became apparent that the 'system' in D.C. was not just going to do the right thing...how to persuade them to act. The result was a legal challenge filed in U.S. Court known as "Ellis vs. EPA"...after nearly 2 years of 'discovery' and 'motions,' is ready to proceed this spring-summer. Bayer, Syngenta and Aventis petitioned the court to be included in the action.

In other parts of the world, full or partial bans are in effect on neonic coated seeds. Results are in, that after its first full year of the ban in the EU the yields on the uncoated seeds were 20% above the ten years' average. In Canada, Ontario is in the process of implementing partial ban while looking at test fields where prescription seeds will be provided according to the demonstrated need for pest control (ex: cutworms.)

Purdue University found no yield difference in using treated seeds. Results are showing a narrow profit margin locally. Farmers need to look at what they are paying for and if they "need" it.

In summary, Steve Ellis asks for testing, a testing process met by due diligence. He stresses that currently, "That's not the case." Since the pesticide coating applied to seeds is currently not considered by EPA as a pesticide application, the treated seeds are deposited nationally over 150 million acres of corn and soybeans. Then there is the concern of the surface water runoff. Is there a connection to the increasing number of diagnosis for autism in our population? We have been told, "It's perfectly tested; it's okay; it's benign." He counters, "Then test more." For example, a form of phosphate has now been determined to be a carcinogen, a substance found in our food. He can't overstate: safety. He would like to see it be guaranteed "safe."

The NRDC issued this statement: "America's bees are dying at some of the highest rates ever recorded, struggling to survive a deluge of toxic pesticides unleashed by multinational chemical giants like Bayer-the world's number 1 manufacturer of bee-killing neonicotinoids...One out of every three bites of food we eat is pollinated by bees—without them the very existence of America's food supply is at stake." Pheasants

Forever publication continues, "Bees and monarchs are critical to human food supplies. A common pesticide, neonic, is synonymous with these insects' demise and rarely does much for farmer yields, according to a report released by the Center for food safety March 24, 2014."

Steven has left for California transporting his bees to facilitate the pollination of the almond crop. One can begin to connect the dots from almonds to apples to pheasants and from California to the grasslands and prairies of the Midwest where both the bees and pheasants feed. There is so much at stake: the concerns of the coating on the seed drifting through the air to other areas, getting into water systems, and reaching into areas designated as "safe spots" for bees. The chemical continues to permeate further. Sussex University, United Kingdom, is finding in their studies that "bees foraging in arable fields are exposed to a complex cocktail of neonicotinoid insecticides and fungicides in the pollen they collect." In this mix the chemical's potency and threat is intensified.

"Listen to the inner voice speaking to you, then dig a little deeper."

Steve Ellis, beekeeper and activist, at Ekberg's home

The Bridge Builder

by Will Allen Dromgoole

An old man going a lone highway,
Came, at the evening cold and gray,
To a chasm vast and deep and wide.
Through which was flowing a sullen tide
The old man crossed in the twilight dim,
The sullen stream had no fear for him;
But he turned when safe on the other side
And built a bridge to span the tide.

"Old man," said a fellow pilgrim near,
"You are wasting your strength with building here;
Your journey will end with the ending day,
You never again will pass this way;
You've crossed the chasm, deep and wide,
Why build this bridge at evening tide?"

The builder lifted his old gray head;
"Good friend, in the path I have come," he said,
"There followed after me to-day
A youth whose feet must pass this way.
This chasm that has been as naught to me
To that fair-haired youth may a pitfall be;
He, too, must cross in the twilight dim;
Good friend, I am building this bridge for him!"

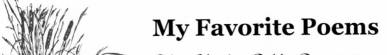

My Favorite Poems

Often Used in Public Presentations,
Funeral Ceremonies and
Inspirational Speeches

A little boy once said to me
What means those three links on your coat
A hidden secret far remote?
They have no hook,
   No snap,
   No bar,
I often wonder what they are.
I thus replied unto that youth,
They are no mystery but Truth,
For enshrined in those three links
Is the Golden Tie that Binds
Men from walks of every kind
If what they teach we would replace,
This sure would be a better place.

One ship sails east
Another sails west
While the self-same breezes blow.
T'is the set of the sail
And not the gale
That bids them where to go
Like the waves of the sea
Are the ways of life
T'is the set of the soul
That decides the goal
And neither the calm nor the strife.

From Jerusalem to Jericho along the great highway,

A lonely wounded traveler in pain and anguish lay.

The thieves had robbed and beaten him and left him there to die

And none were there to offer aid or hear his feeble cry.

The Priest and Levite went in goodly robe and velvet gown on Holy Mission bent.

They saw the wounded traveler but each, although they pitied him, passed on the other side.

From Jerusalem to Jericho there came a good Samaritan who love and mercy had.

He saw the wounded traveler.

He gave him friendly aid and from his scanty purse, his care and lodging paid.

From Jerusalem to Jericho we travel every day,

And many are the wounded ones who lay along the way,

Are you a good Samaritan? Whose love is warm and wide?

Are you like the Holy Ones, who passed on the other side?

If They Should Never Fly

by Richard J. Dorer

If they should never fly again
  Through sunlit skies or mist or rain
Those wary waterfowl that roam
  The heavens' vast uncharted dome -
If in spring's awakening
  The surge of life should fail to bring
A cry of geese or drifting chains
  Of swans upon the trackless lanes -
If from the depth of foggy fen
  The strident call of mallard hen
Were but a thing of memory,
  How dull and drear the spring would be.

If I should lift my eyes on high
  To scan the hazy autumn sky
For migrant fowl, and found no trace,
  Just empty, lifeless, endless space,
If in the sunset's afterglow
  There were no lines to ebb and flow
With thrilling majesty of flight
  Into the shades of coming night -
If that domain to which they cling
  Were lost through ruthless plundering.
Then - truly - they would cease to fly
  And stewardship would wane and die.

Art Gallery and the Golden Plumber Award

Never in my growing up years did it ever occur to me that we might have an art gallery, and yet now it seems like a natural! Well, we got into the business and it did seem to fit. At first we had the Shakopee, Minnesota, Wildlife Art people do our framing because it did not seem possible to do this ourselves with all the other work around the farm and Gay teaching speech therapy at school as well. She enjoyed the work and helping people and did a tremendous amount to correct speech defects. Anyway, I think that with all that we took on it would not be out of order to say that both she and I had vocations.

One of the things that was done at the gallery that we had not counted on at all was feeding people out here in the country. We fed both customers and staff. When people would come to the gallery, they would take a tour and then be hungry so we soon had a snack bar. It quickly became obvious that we needed more than a snack bar and would have to come up with other options for serving food.

People came to see the wild waterfowl in their natural habitat, and soon our children were giving guided tours at an early age (from second grade on up), and were doing a good job of it. We had a fairly attractive display of prints, many of which the artists brought along to the gallery when they came for the Artist Days. Then our gift line increased, giving us an attractive line of small gifts as well as the prints and framed goods.

As time went on, it seemed that the thing to do was to have an art show featuring the art of one or two artists each time. It was on the special artist days that we really had the crowds of people. We had been told not to expect too many people as having an art gallery located out in farming country was a bit unusual. We really appreciated the artists and they liked coming out here for the art shows.

Our attractive farmstead lent itself well to the business of giving tours. We had natural habitat pens that were enhanced by the different species of some very beautiful waterfowl, both ducks and geese. So people would come out to see both the live waterfowl as well as the artwork in the gallery. After taking an hour-long tour, most people were ready to have something to eat. We had acquired a very good Belgian waffle recipe around which we built our food offerings. If a customer wanted a full meal, we served waffles with sausage or bacon. If the preference was a light lunch, the waffle was served with various toppings such as strawberries and whipped cream or whatever berries we had on hand. It worked out very nicely and the people were more than satisfied with the treat. Families who came for the afternoon stayed a few hours to relax and enjoy themselves.

After one rather busy day of serving 20 or more customers, someone asked for another look at a rather popular art print. We checked in the files for the print later that day—lo and behold, it was not there! So after doing an extensive search and failing to locate the item, I had to assume that it was stolen! What to do. There had been a number of people in the gallery that day, some with whom I was not too familiar—could it be possible that one of them had taken the print? This was our first experience with having something taken and it was a very peculiar feeling!

Well, I had all of our staff who had been on hand check again to make sure I had not missed it.

No, it was not there. So that afternoon I called the sheriff. The next morning, the Deputy Sheriff came out from our county seat of Elbow Lake and we went over everything in great detail, and yes indeed, it did seem that things were missing. The deputy suggested that we have our framer, Corlys Behan, do a thorough check of the account books—sure enough, there was more than one item missing. Did we have any suspects? Yes, we did. One of those not-too-familiar people was a traveling print salesman (whom we shall refer to as "Johanson") with whom we had been doing business for a short time. Also, Gay had seen him leaving the gallery suspiciously that day. Customers walk to the gallery and return to their cars in a fairly direct route. However, Johanson stopped by his car, stood still, and stared for a long time. Gay wondered why he was behaving that way. The kids were all in the house, so he had the yard to himself as he stood stock still like a statue. Was he scoping out the yard for any onlookers? Did he have something up his sleeve? It was very peculiar.

While we were doing inventory four or five days after the print allegedly went missing, the phone rang—lo and behold, it was the person who was our prime suspect, Johanson, the not-too-familiar print salesman from the Twin Cities. He was calling to see if we had made up our mind on purchasing some of the prints we had considered on the day he had been here—since it was possibly a rather large order, I had asked for more time to think about placing the order and to talk it over with my wife. Hurrah! How could we be so fortunate to have him call to stop in the next week? Naturally, we would be happy to have him—perhaps he would try his luck and lift some more prints.

As luck would have it, that phone call came in when Deputy Dwight Walvatne was here considering how we should proceed, since there was no link other than our suspicions that Johanson was the culprit. Well, Mr. Johanson was anxious to make a substantial sale and wondered if we would be home the next week—he could make it a point to be here the next Friday at approximately four o'clock in the afternoon.

I said, "Yes, that would be fine." There we had the ideal situation: the suspect coming and hoping to do business—how should we handle this? As Deputy Walvatne said, we could not ask him if he had taken anything because if he had, he was not likely to admit it and would probably leave at once and any further questioning would be out. Our only hope would be that if he had gotten away with prints before, hopefully he might try it again. But we had to be so careful not to say or do anything that would even border on "entrapment."

Now, we had no way of knowing what kind of a person we were dealing with in the person of Johanson. Was he a hardened criminal? Did he carry a gun? Or was he a gentle soul? We really were wondering, because the sheriff's office could find nothing on him or any kind of a record. What really made us wonder were that the facts seemed to bear out he may have stolen before from us. We had discovered that an expensive print was missing and turned up in an art gallery in Florida. We could tell this because every print has its own number, and from the record somehow there was a print with our number on it in Florida. So how big of a deal was this? One print alone was worth $700!

Well, we decided to play it by ear and see what would happen. We decided we would try to get him to unknowingly visit with Deputy Walvatne when he came. The deputy decided he would not use a sheriff's car nor wear a uniform, and there might possibly be other customers present so he would not give any hint that he was a law officer. Actually, Dwight dressed as a plumber!

Well, the big day was at hand. I was as nervous as could be, not knowing what the suspect was like. Four o'clock came and the kids got off the bus and sure enough as the time approached here came a car around the lake, up the driveway, and parked next to the gallery. The school bus had delivered our children and the next person scheduled to arrive was Gay returning from teaching school. The kids were aware that the suspect was in the art gallery visiting with Deputy Walvatne, who from all outward appearances was a plumber. Then Gay drove in and nine-year-old Joel ran to meet her, shouting, "Mom, Mom, the suspect is in the gallery!"

Johanson had no idea he was talking to a deputy, and obviously he did not hear what Joel had just said. Gay got the kids into the house with her and I went into the gallery to visit with the suspect, who was just winding down his visit with the deputy. Johanson did not suspect anything and immediately launched into his sales pitch with me. Dwight made a beeline to the house and advised Gay to let the kids play outside, that everything should appear as normal. Johanson had a large print folder in his hands that he had brought with him and was really chattering away. I was as nervous as a cat on a hot tin roof. It's funny that the suspect didn't hear my heart pounding.

Hey, did that rascal Johanson, the suspect, just slip one of our big prints into one of his big file folders? I was so rattled that I didn't know what was going on. *Whoops! I believe he just slipped another print into the folder.* Things were happening so fast with Johanson talking a mile a minute and excitedly waving his arms that I was completely bewildered and didn't trust what I was hearing or seeing. I was stressed out and a wreck. Johanson was in command of the situation and packed up to go. I followed Johanson out of the gallery, where he packed up his car and hit the road. Dwight came over to me and said that, from his vantage point when Johanson was talking to me, he had seen a couple more prints go into the folder. After Johanson left, Dwight told me he had counted 13 missing pieces.

Dwight then called the sheriff and told him to have the other deputy pick up Johanson and arrest him. The other deputy was at a strategic location along the road we anticipated Johanson would take to return to the Cities. Then Dwight and the other deputy stopped Johanson. Initially, Dwight asked to see the folder under Johanson's arm and Johanson agreed he could search the car.

But when Dwight again asked to inspect the folder under Johanson's arm, a tussle ensued. They were yanking the folder back and forth until finally Dwight won out and claimed the folder, which indeed did have a number of prints—some of which we were not aware Johanson had taken and were a complete shock to us. Dwight then arrested the thief.

Then we went to court, where Johanson was charged with theft. He showed no remorse or guilt. Our lawyer said that Johanson had ice water in his veins. The end result was that we got the merchandise returned from this attempt, but none from the first theft.

This was a highlight of Dwight Walvatne's career; for being so innovative, the law enforcement crew presented him with the "Golden

Plumber Award." It was a bathroom plunger painted gold and attached to a base—such a prominent award that it was pictured in the local newspaper!

Not connected, but still an award—in 1990 the Lake Region Arts Council presented the Lawndale Gallery with one of its annual awards of recognition, an artist's engraved ceramic plate for the wall.

Gay and Gordon (far right) received an award from Lake Region Arts Council for art promotion at Lawndale Farm, where the "rushes and the brushes" meet.

"Many of the state's and nation's major wildlife artists ... painters such as Dan Smith and Jim Hautman ... have used Lawndale for research for their paintings. The artists photograph waterfowl and habitat as some of the models in their paintings. The list of artists goes past twenty. The arts council said, 'Gordon and his wife Gay have created a business that enhances the environment, the art world, and the lifestyle of our region.'"
— *Herman Review*, August 1990

Photo Gallery

Frank and Augusta Ekberg family with children Irven, Oscar, Walter, Effie and Ray

Isaak (aka Isak, Isaac) and Johana (aka Johanna) (Gustafson) Ekberg, Gordon's great-grandparents from Smaland, Sweden

Frank Ekberg

Mrs. Ekberg

Frank Ekberg Was Early Settler

F. A. Ekberg, father of Irven Ekberg of Herman, was one of this community's early settlers. The following history is taken from an account that was written in his own hand prior to his passing, January 1, 1953.

F. A. Ekberg was born in Traheryd County, Smoland, Sweden June 16, 1858. He came to Herman in November 1875 and spent the rest of his life here. In his early years here he worked on area farms, clerked in C. Johnson's General Store in Evansville for one year, and clerked for John Christianson and Winger Co. Store in Herman for five years.

On January 23, 1885 he was married to Augusta W. Peterson and in 1886 they moved on the homestead that was to become known as the Axel Gilbertson farm. In 1900 he built up on the farm where his grandson, Gordon Ekberg, now lives. He lived there until 1924 when his son, the late Walter Ekberg, assumed management of the family farm and Frank and Agusta Ekberg moved into Herman. Their home for the next 14 years was in a large frame dwelling located where the Herman Review now stands. On May 25, 1938 Mrs. Ekberg died and Frank moved back to the farm. He lived with his son Walter and family until his death in 1953.

Frank Ekberg was on the Macsville Town Board for over 35 years and served as Assessor for 12 years. Other official duties included: School Board Clerk for 35 years, Farmers Elevator Board, Herman Creamery Board, Board of County Commissioners, Grant County Fair Board, Grant County Bank Board, Delaware Insurance Board, and the Herman Cemetery Board. He was also a member of the Board of Deacons of Bethel Lutheran Church for over 50 years.

*Frank
Ekberg
obituary*

~ 95 ~

Aunt Effie dressed special with fine clothes, jewelry, hats and furs

Grandpa Ekberg going to church

*Wedding of
Anna and Henry Gord*

*Henry Gord
with daughters
Helen and Della*

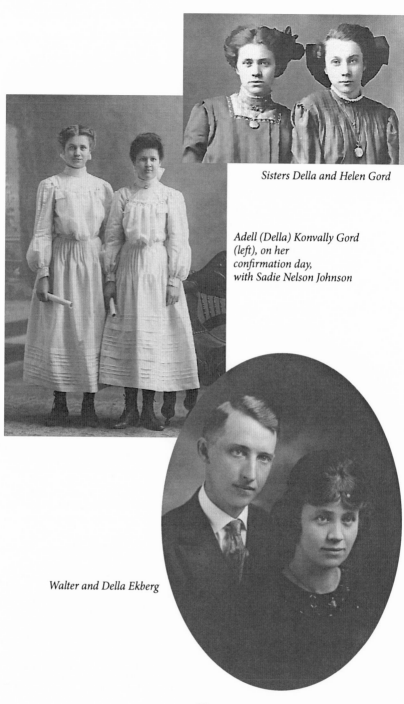

Sisters Della and Helen Gord

Adell (Della) Konvally Gord
(left), on her
confirmation day,
with Sadie Nelson Johnson

Walter and Della Ekberg

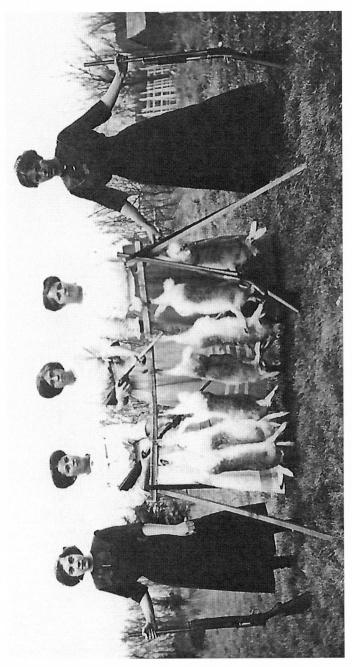

Helen and Della Gord (far left and far right) helped bring in several large jackrabbits from a road known as "Jackrabbit Road" because of the large white jackrabbits sighted in the winter.

*Walter Ekberg with his
prize-winning cornstalk*

*Walter and Adell Ekberg (1947)
25th wedding anniversary*

A candid shot of the Walter Ekberg family

Gordon Through the Years

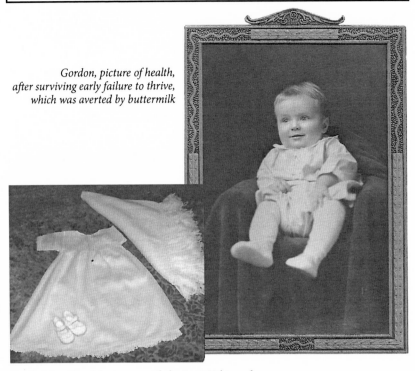

Gordon, picture of health,
after surviving early failure to thrive,
which was averted by buttermilk

Gordon's baptismal dress was made by Aunt Helen and worn
by his five children and two grandchildren. Shawl was made by
friend Joan Adams.

Beloved
Grandpa
Henry
Gord
holding
up
little
Gordon
by the
once-
screened-
in porch

*One-year-old
Gordon with
his dad Walter
in the doorway
of the smaller
porch*

*Jean, Grandma Augusta Ekberg
and Gordon (they can both
remember sitting on her lap while
she peeled an apple for them)*

*Cousin
Jean
Ekberg
with
Gordon*

*Gordon
in his
highchair*

*Little Gordon
in his sailor outfit*

*Young Gordon
perched on a
ladder*

*Gordon with
grandparents
Frank and
Augusta
Ekberg*

Gordon as a young lad wearing knickers, which he detested

above: Gordon riding his new bicycle, one of the first in this area

below: Gordon on his tricycle by the lilac hedge, which kept dust from the nearby road off the yard

Gordon feeding a kitty

Gordon and Spot as he builds a topper for his wagon

Young Gordon with favorite dog, Spot, who saved Gordon's life when ill and needing companionship and motivation

Young Gordon

Gordon pulling a wagon that he modified to haul branches

Grandpa Gord and Gordon

School photo

Gordon and Spot on his seesaw using his imagination and Spot's devoted cooperation

Gordon with Polly, the pony that saved his life
in the 1941 Armistice Day Storm

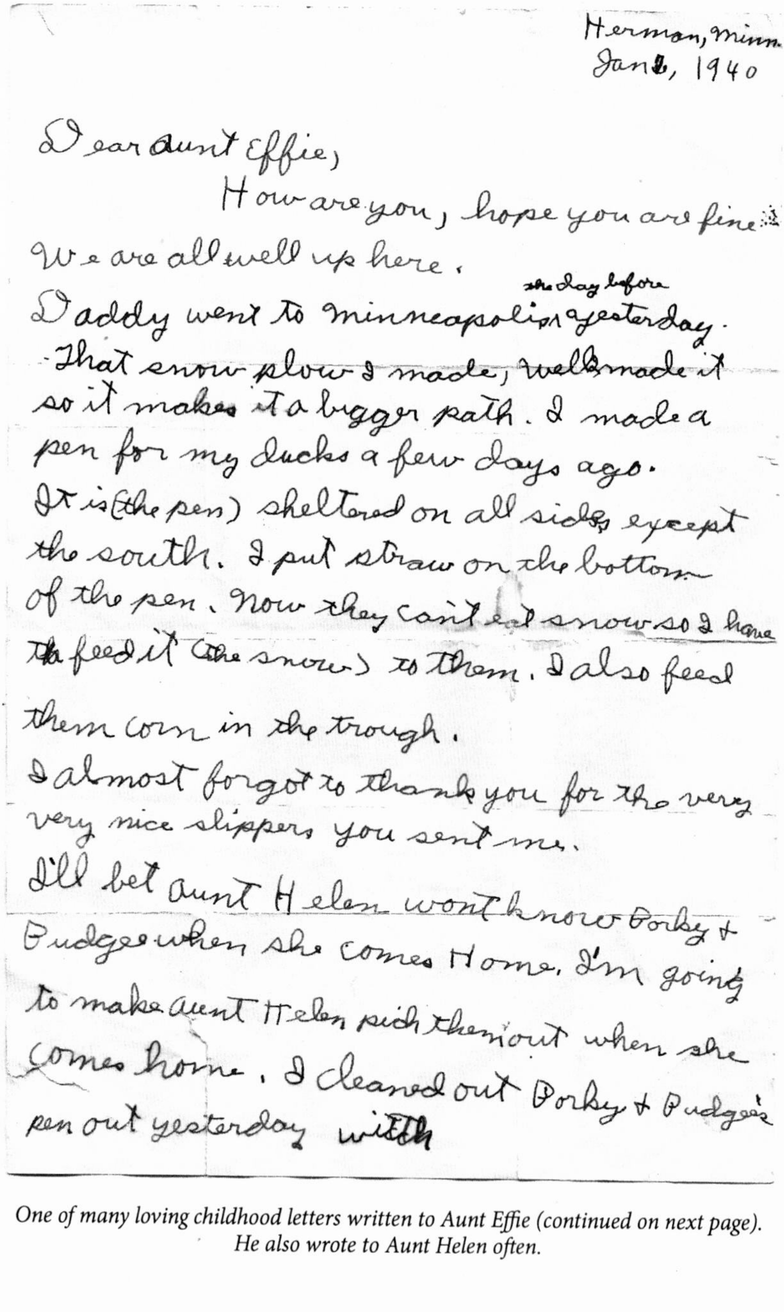

Herman, Minn.
Jan 1, 1940

Dear aunt Effie,

How are you, hope you are fine.
We are all well up here.
Daddy went to Minneapolis the day before yesterday.
That snow plow I made, well made it
so it makes it a bigger path. I made a
pen for my ducks a few days ago.
It is (the pen) sheltered on all sides except
the south. I put straw on the bottom
of the pen. Now they can't eat snow so I have
to feed it (the snow) to them. I also feed
them corn in the trough.
I almost forgot to thank you for the very
very nice slippers you sent me.
I'll bet aunt Helen won't know Porky &
Pudge when she comes home. I'm going
to make aunt Helen pick them out when she
comes home. I cleaned out Porky & Pudge's
pen out yesterday with

One of many loving childhood letters written to Aunt Effie (continued on next page).
He also wrote to Aunt Helen often.

Hasn't been cleaned out since christmas,
So I opened the door & chased them out & were
they tickled to get out. I cleaned the pen out & put
in clean straw witch I put in 3 feet deep in 1 corner
& gave them corn in a trough. I have another
cold & bad cough. We took down the christmas
tree Tuesday. They still have the tree in the
Church, Irvin Fabian was here till last night

We didn't celeabrate New years Day this
year.
Thank you again for the nice slippers
Well thats all I can think of.

your nephew

Gordon

Hugs & Kisses } from Gordon
0 0 0 + X X X

Gordon in the blue winter suit, one he didn't care for. His cousin Jean had an identical red one, gifts from their doting aunt.

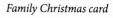

Family Christmas card

Best Christmas Wishes and Happiness throughout the year

Gordon with a 17-pound northern
he caught at Cliff Hanson's

Gordon as a youth

Gordon and his raccoon,
a pet that washed its food
in water before eating

Gordon with kittens and Spot by long porch

The Reuss neighbor advised Gordon to make a martin house to eradicate the mosquitos in the yard. At age 16, Gordon built a substantial martin birdhouse, and it still stands in place today.

Gordon's pets: the Airedale with the raccoon rescued from a neighbor's attic

Gordon and his parents
(Photo taken by Aunt Verna Ekberg)

Gordon between cousins Marilyn and Eileen Ekberg

Gordon Ekberg-Biography

*Address: Herman, Minnesota 56248

*Age: 47

*Married: Two Children

*Methodist: Lay Pastor and Sunday School Teacher

*Farmer: 560 acres of land
Crops: wheat, barley, beans, and corn
Livestock: hogs (major), cattle, sheep

*DFL: Active for over 25 years — precinct chairman, fund chairman County Central Committee, Chairman of Senator Wayne Olhoft Volunteer Committee, and Representative Carl Iversen Volunteer Committee.

*Member: Farmers Union — 25 years plus.

*Member: National Farmers Organization — County President, Secretary, Public Relations, writes monthly column, extensive speaking engagements.

*Member: Odd Fellow Lodge — Past Grand Master of Minnesota (Outstanding Grand Master North American Continent, 1963, International Officer, 1970, Representative of Minnesota to International Convention, 6 years).

*Member: American Angus Association
American Simmetal Association
Columbia Sheep Breeders Association of America

*Honorary Member: Future Farmers of America.

*Dale Carnegie Graduate.

*Served in the Following Offices: Township Clerk, 8 years
First President, County Assn. Twp. Officers
County Red Cross, 3 years
Lakeside Cemetery Assoc., Director 15 years
County Farmers Home Administration, 3 years (President, 1 year)
President and Secretary, Herman Investment Club

*Hobbies: Raising Wild Waterfowl
Camping, Hunting, Fishing, and Trapping.

Gordon's campaign flyer when running for the DFL endorsement for Representative in the United States Congress for the Seventh District, Minnesota.
Ten days after Bob Bergland accepted the appointment as Secretary of Agriculture, several candidates expressed their interest to run for his vacated seat (December 1976).

One of Gordon's campaign photos

Gordon making breakfast for the children before school – one of many

Evening of jewel presentations at Harmony Lodge, IOOF (1991)
front: guest, Art Bengtson, Carl Niemackl, Neil Hanson
back: Walter McRoberts, Wally Andersen, Roger Andersen, Gordon and Les Asmus

Major Gordon Ekberg (right), member of IOOF semi-military branch, the Canton (also known as Patriarchs Militant promoting peace and soldierly valor)

l-r: Sovereign Grand Master Don Smith (California), Dr. Jim Lombard (chairman) and Gordon Ekberg working on S.G.L. film committee

A group of deer hunters who went north of Thief River Falls, Minnesota, for several days of deer hunting in November. Gordon was one of the people to initiate the annual hunt near Four Town, complete with tent and home-cooked meals.

Gordon giving his acceptance speech after receiving the Pioneer Conservationist of the Year at the Waterfowl Association banquet (clipping from Grant County Herald, *2/18/87). (Photo by Steve Kufrin, Editor,* Minnesota Waterfowler *magazine) Joe Alexander, DNR Commissioner, left, was a featured speaker at the event.*

Gordon by his waterfowl pens, taken by a semi-professional photographer guest. Gordon said it was his "best picture" – that is how he really looked!

opposite: An ad where Gordon is an example of successful telemedicine videoconference, consulting from Elbow Lake with a cardiologist at Abbott Northwestern Hospital, and resulting in a needed trip to Abbott-Northwestern for an emergency angioplasty. The telemedicine network sponsored by Allina Health System and Rural Health Alliance in partnership with U S WEST, gave Gordon a new lease on life.

Gordon at Red Rock Lake National Wildlife Refuge at Lima, Montana, at swan nest site – ready to put five eggs into suitcase (1982)

Gordon with neighbor Marge Andersen, celebrating his first big outing (after Jan-Feb hospitalization) at Stella's, Battle Lake (Spring 2016) (Photo by Gay Ekberg)

Gordon with physical therapist in first walk across the yard after a few months of home therapy; he was so happy to learn he was able to do this (2016).

Gordon at Hoffman Harvest Festival parade

Gordon when first introduced to editor Joy Minion at Mable Murphy's, Fergus Falls (Fall 2016). He is telling about his trips to Alaska and showing items from those trips.

Gordon writing his story at the dining room table

Final Footnote for the extra 11 years of life allocated to Gordon to accomplish his book.
Eleven years ago, Gordon's health failed: his steps were short, he suffered incontinence and had a short memory. John saw an ad on TV describing the same symptoms. Taking printed online information to the family doctor and insisting this is what Gordon had, Dr. Rapp referred Gordon to neurologist in Fergus Falls, who promptly sent him to Abbott-Northwestern Hospital to specialist Dr. McCue in the Piper Building. Dr. McCue performs 50 surgeries per year for NPH (normal pressure hydrocephalus), inserting a shunt to relieve water on the brain. A risky surgery, but when Gordon said he wanted to write a book, Dr. McCue agreed to help him get the book written. The surgery was a success and symptoms were reversed. Gordon did complete his book about a week before he passed away. As Gordon stated on page 22, in the ending statement of "Close Calls on My Life": I am hoping to finish this book!

Cemetery stone, decorated Memorial Day weekend for Gordon

Lawndale Farm Through the Years

Frank Ekberg home before the west end was added on. This house was built shortly after 1900. We know that Grandpa Peterson (father of Augusta Peterson Ekberg) built the kitchen cabinets and a bedroom closet, and perhaps more.
Labor and material for the house came to $500.
A large picture window and beautiful open staircase were very special features.

The home with awnings back when Aunt Effie shared the home with Walter and Della. "She loved it there." (about 1940)

The early Lawndale Farm— the barn and buildings were initially painted red; white in later years.

Hip roof barn, particular to that time, entering Lawndale Farm

Lawndale Farm home (2010)

above & below: Ponds made in the seven- acre section of the pond owned by Gordon.
During a dry year, Gordon hired Vernell Wagner to build 22 islands
plus a dike cordoning off his section. The islands were to protect nesting birds
from predators, a virtual safe haven.
While Vernell dug two feet deeper around each island, in one corner of this pond
he dug another three-four feet to form a possible fish pond.

In digging, some interesting observations occurred.
In that deepest area of digging, there were two feet of black soil on top.
Next was a layer of rushes, followed by two feet of dirt with snails.
There was a final layer of rushes topping off one foot of dirt.
The very bottom was sand, perhaps the original lake bed.

Gordon went over the islands with a Melroe drag
after seeding it with various vegetation by hand.

The series of pens developed to maintain waterfowl in a safe environment, protected from predators on ground and overhead. The background structure is the canvasback pen, modeled after the one of its kind in Canada (1983).

One of the several duck pens holding a variety of species, with protective netting overhead and protective fabric dug several inches into the ground at the fenceline to keep predators out. These pens were a popular feature for many educational tours.

Emperor Geese, collected as eggs in the wild of Alaska, later becoming the models for Dan Smith's winning entry into Alaska's First of State duck stamp contest. "The geese are among nearly 900 waterfowl that make their home at the farm owned by Gordon and Gay Ekberg." (Oct. 15,1987, Country Life, supplement to the Fergus Falls Daily Journal) Photo by Coleen Neumann

Trumpeter swans at Lawndale Farm

Whitetail deer at Lawndale Farm

Farm site at the Lawndale Environmental Foundation
(former Aurora and Peter/Judy Noreen home sites)

Lawndale Farm swan post card (above & below) – the idea that lead to the gift shop and eventually to the print shop, frame shop, B&B, art gallery and Belgian waffle restaurant. The photo was taken by Charles Hanson, Correll, Minnesota. The cattail logo was created by Michelle Heiberg.

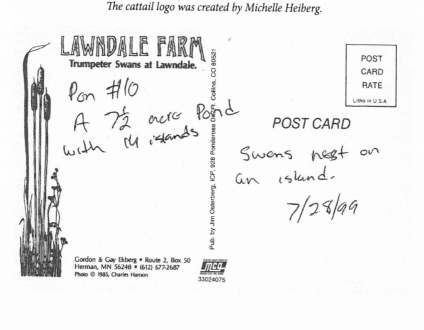

Gordon and Gay with guest artists Michael Sieve, Donna Torgerson, and Daniel Smith

Kenneth and Evelyn Morrel served funnel cakes on the fields at Lawndale Farm for Prairie days. Gordon gave tours to people on a hayrack over fields, through prairie and around marshes.

Gay and Gordon Ekberg

Photo from one of the newspaper articles saved by Gordon's mother-in-law in her scrapbook regarding 15 years in B&B business

Gordon with a wildlife art print that he framed and hung in the gallery (January 1986 newspaper clipping)

Daniel Smith by his painting "Where Eagles Fly"
during an artist day at the art gallery.
"He said he has been to Lawndale Farm three or four times during the past year,
to photograph the Ekberg's birds and to observe them closely. The emperor geese
(below) that will be on the Alaska duck stamp and the wood ducks that will be on
the Georgia duck stamp are both modeled after birds at the Ekberg's farm."
(October 1984, newspaper clipping)

"The first of state Alaskan Duck Stamp print painted by Daniel Smith. The Emperor Geese from Lawndale Farm were the models for the picture and helped him to win the duck stamp competition."
(October 1984, newspaper clipping)
One of these geese is yet present in the art gallery, among the taxidermy work.

"...very few people bring the concern and enthuslasm that Gordon brings to it."...Bruce Batt.

Gordon referring to the waterfowl area during an interview.
Gordon and Gay Ekberg were among 168 farm families to be recognized in the
Successful Farming *magazine's Farming in the Flyways program.*
"In cooperation with the Mid-Continent restoration program, the Ekbergs restored 7
marshes on their land ... planted 77 acres of their land into switchgrass.
They put 14 acres of land into the Water Bank program, planted 5 acres for wildlife plot,
and planted 3,000 trees, including an 8 ½ mile single row windbreak."
(February 22, 1990, Herman Review)
(Photo by Steven Kufrin, Minnesota Waterfowler *publication)*

The prairie area Gordon developed on farmland,
full of flowers to support the bees in honey production

Sharon Wald presenting her popular scratchboard art at Lawndale Farm Wildlife Gallery. "*Scratchboard artist Sharon Wald displayed her work at last Saturday, October 13. Her unique work, the result of scratching through black paint to layers of colored paint below, uses wildlife and flowers as its subject matter. She said that she is now experimenting with backgrounds made of collages and torn paper, although what sells best, she says, are her paintings of wildlife.*"*(From October 1984,* Herman Review *newspaper clipping)*

"*Ekberg also has a frame shop on his farm.*" *From newspaper clipping titled* "*More than just a gallery*" *(1986)*

Nationally-known artist Mario Fernandez drawing a remarque on his print "A Place that Time Forgot" (birds by an abandoned church steeple), on location at the art gallery (1980s)

Bruce Burk in our yard in June 1983. He is an author, photographer and decoy carver from California who wrote a series of books in volumes called Complete Waterfowl Studies, *and included birds he photographed at Lawndale Farm, giving credit in the book to Gordon.*

Terry Redlin visited in February 1985 and signed the canvas "guest board" kept for signatures of visiting artists. Terry wrote: Great Place! Be back again.

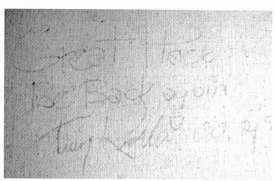

Michael Sieve, big game artist, drew a remarque on the canvas guest board.

Among other well-known artist guests were Jimmy and Bob Hautman, "the Hautman Brothers."

Friends and nationally-known artists Mario Fernandez and Jim Meger, sharing an art show at Lawndale Farm Wildlife Gallery.

Gordon, representing the Lawndale Environmental Foundation, was a guest speaker at the Wildlife and Western Art Exhibit, Minneapolis, April 1989. About 10,000 people attended the show and volunteers for the Foundation passed out 3,000 brochures to the public.

December, 1988

Gay and Gordon Ekberg
Lawndale Farm
Route 2, Box 50
Herman, Minnesota 56248

Dear Gay and Gordon:

I would like to congratulate you on your outstanding work in the Bed and Breakfast industry. As you well know, the B&B industry is expanding and prospering in Minnesota.

Minnesota's long tradition of generosity and hospitality provides the perfect atmosphere for the B&B industry. People like you keep that tradition going strong.

I am a strong supporter of B&Bs and our office recently sent a mailing to media statewide promoting the accomplishments of the industry in Minnesota. The mailing contained a fact sheet from the Office of Tourism and a letter from myself.

I have enclosed the letter I sent to the editors, the fact sheet, a copy of the proclamation I presented at a recent Bed and Breakfast conference, and an article recently published by the Star & Tribune newspaper, which I found to be very encouraging for the Bed and Breakfast industry.

I wish you success with your Bed and Breakfast and best of luck in all your endeavors.

Sincerely,

RUDY PERPICH
Governor

AN EQUAL OPPORTUNITY EMPLOYER

Commendation to Gordon and Gay for operating new Bed&Breakfast, written by Minnesota Governor Rudy Perpich (December 1988).

Matt Olhoft, on behalf of the Grant County Farm Bureau,
presenting Century Farm Award to Gordon and Gay (2002)

Jim Meger drawing a remarque on his print of pheasants at the art gallery

above & below: The lily pad pond built by Gordon and the boys for Gay (a fan of Claude Monet's work). Gordon added cattails and bulrushes in the far end.

Gordon, "A Natural" as Teacher of Environmental Education

Gordon teaching environmental class to
3rd graders at Herman school.
He related so well to students and
kept their rapt attention. (1990)

Gordon's classroom presentation
about animals and their fur pelts
(September 24, 1992)

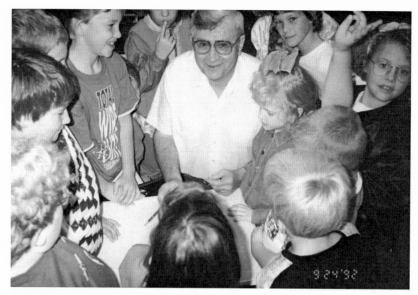

Gordon surrounded by Herman third graders during an environmental lesson

Environmental lesson at Lawndale Farm

Gordon and Gay Ekberg were married on December 23, 1972, at the Methodist Church in Herman, MN. Pastor Lloyd Osborn presided. The wedding cake was made by Mrs. Johnson.

(Gordon was filling pulpit for Pastor Osborn when he first saw Gay in the congregation in June 1971. Gordon preached at the church for three months while Pastor Lloyd recovered from a heart attack.)

Gay Derby, summer of 1972, at Gordon's Uncle Irven and Aunt Verna's lake home on Lake Minnewaska

below:
Honeymoon photo taken at Daytona Beach, Florida

Children's first day of school, 1983
l-r: Kris Ann, Joel, Amy)

Kris Ann riding a horse near Red Rock Lake, Montana, where Gordon's family
was one of six families in the U.S. allowed to secure a clutch of five swan eggs
and attempt to raise them in captivity.

Gay and Vangie, age three

Children's first day of school, 1988
back: Kris Ann, Amy
middle: Joel
front: Vangie and John

Oldest daughter Kris Ann Konvally Ekberg by
her English spot garden, something Gordon
encouraged each child to develop after visiting
Chapel Gardens at Eagle Bend (operated by
Eva Schroeder).

*The bumper crop of pumpkins Gordon raised one year
with Joel, Kris Ann, Vangie, and Amy (mid-1980s)*

*John's project on fur trading for sixth grade, with Gordon's assistance.
No chart or small display would do – Gordon insisted on building the whole trading post
and took up a part of the school gymnasium.*

Gordon and Gay
Joel, Amy and
Kris Ann at
Hall of Fame event

Joel, Gordon
and John

John, Gordon and Joel at deer camp

Family Christmas card photo

Gordon and Gay's 25th wedding anniversary celebrated in Appleton, Wisconsin, where Kris Ann was working

*Pictured in the University of Minnesota-Report for working with
the Small Business Resource Center and the Grants, Development,
and Regional Programs Office at the Morris campus.
They help entrepreneurs like Gordon Ekberg who will provide a sanctuary for rare and
endangered waterfowl. Gordon is holding a rare Siberian red-breasted duck.*

Gordon and Gay

Gordon and Gay at her 30ᵗʰ high school class reunion at the Herman restaurant

Gordon and Gay (2016)

Invitation designed by Vangie Ekberg Johnson for her parents 140th birthday party
(Gordon – 80, Gay – 60)

WHAT: Gordon Ekberg is turning 80 and Gay is turning 60 this year. Your familiy is invited to celebrate their combined 140 years!

WHERE: Lawndale Farm
15197 240th Avenue
Herman, MN 56248

WHEN: Saturday, June 20th, starting at 2pm there will be appetizers and beverages. 5:30pm there will be a short program and cake, a bonfire after dark (weather permitting). Come for all or part of the day.

We would like to put together a memory book for Gordon and Gay, please send your favorite memory and/or photo of them to Amy by either email (Splippy66@hotmail.com) or snail mail by June 4:

Amy Ekberg
2008 Grand Ave. #106
St. Paul, MN 55105

1451 Schletti Street
St. Paul, MN 55117

Gay and Gordon on their joint 140th birthday party (60 years and 80 years, respectively). About 300 people came to visit, eat and listen to two bands play under a tent (Rodney Koser singing old time with his accordion & Ryan Smith with new time on guitar). The two bands alternated each half hour throughout the day.

Gay made it to Paris (August 2009) after her 60th birthday party in June

Drawing Kris Ann made for her father

Gay Ekberg and Maxine Adams, LRAC staff, hold a photo of Gordon as Gay accepts the the fully-funded grant for Gordon's book on his behalf.
December 15, 2016, at the LRAC office, Fergus Falls

Family Events and Memories

Those Were the Days!

Our older children did many things that made us so proud, and then later the younger ones did the same! At an early age, Kris Ann and Amy served as tour guides. What were they guiding? Tours of our natural habitat bird pens, which at one time held 57 species of waterfowl from around the world. Many were the comments after visitors completed the tour, expressing amazement regarding the knowledge and professional manner that our two little girls demonstrated. During the tour, both could answer the most difficult and technical questions that the guests could muster up. They also helped in keeping the pens neat and clean.

A few years later, with the opening of a restaurant/art gallery on the farm, the girls waited the tables serving Belgian Waffles and other goodies. They also answered many questions about the pictures framed and on display in the art gallery section, some of which were pictures of the many birds on site. Joel also became a tour guide and a right-hand man in feeding birds and helping with all the upkeep. Once in a while an artist would leave an original painting and that would cause excitement and many questions.

Just lately, our younger son John, who has taken over the gallery, was having a phone conversation concerning the activities and business of over 30 years ago with a nationally known artist, Dan Smith. During the phone conversation, Dan remarked, "Those were the days!" Dan and his family used to come up to photograph birds and put on a show. The tone of his voice in that remark registered admiration and respect, which

Gay and I very much appreciated. We have really enjoyed having the artists, and the artists enjoyed coming here, especially when Gay fixed their favorite noon meal. For a period of three or four years we had about 20-30 people every weekend and when we had an "Art Show" we had as many as 300 visitors. It was a lot of work, but we all enjoyed it!

Through the years, I have always had a particular closeness to one set of cousins because we grew up geographically close, about two miles apart, and that is truly an asset. We went to the same school together, as well as to the same church and Youth Group. My cousins used to visit often—the big attraction at that time was two large American Elm trees on our front lawn that supported a nice large hammock. We manually gave swinging hammock rides to the cousins!

To me, who has no living siblings, that has been so meaningful as it seems more like a brother/sister relationship than that of cousins. (Jean Rae, Eileen Mae and Marilyn Janice, I hope this does not embarrass you.) Then there are my more distant cousins, the late Irma Faye of California, and Millie Rae and her late brother John Robert of Montevideo, Minnesota—these three also hold a special place in my heart. We opened our home to Grandpa Frank Ekberg for 14 years after my grandmother passed. Also making their home with us were Aunt Effie (my dad's sister) and Aunt Helen (my mother's sister.) The aunts made their living away from here, Effie by teaching school and Helen by doing housekeeping. But for all of that time, each of them received a weekly letter written by my mother.

One of the interesting things that we, the Gordon and Gay Ekberg family, did was to write and direct a very special life-like presentation of the Nativity Play at church before Christmas. One highlight was the entrance of our son Joel, who at ten years of age played the part of an angel who flew through a small distance supported by a series of ropes and pulleys to bring the message of the coming Christ Child's Birth. It was quite unique and effective. We also arranged for the Wisemen to follow a moving star.

When we decided to go out to the National Bird Convention at Cody, Wyoming, near Yellowstone National Park, Gay's mother, Grace

Derby, went along to help with 10- month old Vangie, Joel, and the other two girls. We had rented a motorhome at Pierre, South Dakota. Driving through the mountains with a motorhome whose brakes were failing was a never-to-be-forgotten experience, to say the least. One morning we were going to have pancakes for breakfast and when turning a sharp corner, the syrup bottle fell off the counter, broke into pieces on the rug and made a general mess of things. It seemed to take forever to get it clean.

We were one of only six families in the United States given permission to collect a clutch of swan eggs from the wild. A gentleman from Wisconsin offered to share a ride with us to Red Rock Lake National Wildlife Refuge in southwest Montana to get a setting of swan eggs. This offer of a ride was great. However, we were constantly on pins and needles because of his speed on the winding mountain roads, 100 miles per hour! We were taken by Refuge manager Gene Stroops in a boat to the nest. We collected the five eggs, put them into a suitcase filled with eiderdown and hot water bottles, and indeed did speed for home to get the eggs safely incubated under bantam hens.

Another memory involves orange juice. I enjoy orange juice, but I had a tough time regulating my consumption of it. In later years, after numerous trips to the doctor's office, I ended up at the Mayo Clinic in Rochester where it was discovered that I was sensitive to orange juice in the quantity that I had unwisely consumed. It cost me $7,000 to have the doctors at Mayo tell me of my sensitivity to large amounts of orange juice. Most people have the sense to consume in moderation. I should have had a clue, because as a child I was constantly asking for oranges. My aunt said that at a very young age, I constantly brought this to my folks' attention by demands of "More oranges, more oranges." I mention it because it is something that caused a great deal of concern in my life. My symptoms seemed to duplicate those of my father-in-law, whose symptoms were those of terminal cancer.

Collecting swan eggs – Amy (hidden), Kris Ann, Gay and Gordon at Red Rock Lake National Wildlife Refuge near Lima, Montana

The five swan eggs collected from a nest on Red Rock Lake, Montana. The clutch of five eggs was transferred from Montana back to Lawndale Farm by Gordon in his eider-down-filled suitcase. Four hatched into cygnets (baby trumpeter swans).

The Sheriff's Car

Was It Levitating? Yeah!

I joined the NFO the same night as I embarked on my duties as Grand Master of the Odd Fellows of Minnesota. Either one was a substantial load—how I ever managed to do a good job of both, I'll never know, but people said that I had. I had not anticipated doing anything more for the NFO than paying my dues, but I was also asked to publicly speak for that organization as well. Things did seem to work out all right.

I well remember the evening I signed my membership contract with the NFO. I had felt for many years that the farmer needed a stronger voice in pricing his commodities on the retail market as well as the bulk market. I felt I would be a good NFO member and pay my dues and attend the monthly meetings, but it did not turn out that way. They soon had me in as the county secretary and then as public relations officer, so I was in the thick of activities before I was aware of what was going on. I also helped out on smaller committees. I met and appreciated so many good people. After going to a few meetings and meeting people, I soon discovered that there were also people, who for whatever reason, did not like the NFO. As time went on I increased my circle of acquaintances and friends.

Then one day they decided to ask the National Tea Packing Plant in Fergus Falls to sign a contract with the NFO or shut down. Well, that stirred a number of people up and I didn't know what was going to happen. One afternoon the president of the First National Bank in Herman called me on the telephone and said that a friend of his who didn't believe in the NFO was going up to National Tea at Fergus with about three 240-pound hogs in his pickup just to show that he could still get in. You see the rumor was out that the NFO was going to try and shut National Tea down, which meant that the NFO was going to try to blockade the National Tea Plant so no farmer could deliver hogs to National Tea. The farmers who didn't like NFO were going to run the blockade down.

This concerned me, because the farmer who told the banker what he was going to do was also a friend of mine. I was quite sure that if he had said he was going through the blockade with three hogs—and if necessary run right into the blockade, no matter who got hurt—well, knowing the person, I was quite sure that he might do such a thing. The appointed time was at sunrise the next morning so I at first thought, *No, I'll just let it go.* When I found out that a number of people were going up from our area, I thought I had better go also to try to subdue the antagonistic attitude.

The NFO Meat Board Chairman had called and told me he was picking me up at sunrise that next morning, so I had better be ready to go at that time and I was. We got up to Fergus Falls just as the sun was coming up. There were about 200 NFO members there with more coming all the time. With a couple of members that I came with, we went over to the office to talk with management. I was asked to go to the entrance where the NFO was congregating along with the sheriff and three deputies.

I stuck my head in the sheriff's car, which had people packed around it like sardines. I thought that the car containing the sheriff and his three deputies was raising while I was partly in the car. It was at that moment I positively detected that the sheriff's car was being raised off the ground by the NFO people. The young deputies were terrified to hear members of the crowd saying, "Lift the car up and shake the officers out!"

The car was now about 2 ½ to 3 feet in the air. It was then that I used my loudest and most commanding voice to say, "Put it back on the ground!"

Slowly the car started to lower. It was a terrifying moment and one in which anything could have happened; fear ran rampant with "mob" rule. I noted trousers were soiled due to fear and I wasn't that far from soiling clothes myself. Well, the car finally met the ground as the officers scrambled out of it! We ordered everyone to "go home" and that miraculously happened. I do not care to be exposed to "mob" rule, and I had said a prayer under my breath—and I think others had too.

Another time I was asked to speak to the Wright County NFO and ask that they pay their dues because there were over 750 members owing back dues for two or more years. I am not sure how it happened that I was contacted to see what I could do. I had been accepting speaking engagements as I had time to do so and often it just worked out that way. I can't remember that much of the details of the large amount of back dues. It seems to me that there had been something commented on by the Catholic National Rural Life organization down in Iowa.

Richard Rung had been hauling me around in the back seat of his car while I caught up on some much needed sleep. It seems that I had been doing some speaking in Fargo, North Dakota, area and it came up where they wanted me to speak at Wright County. After speaking in the Fargo area, while I slept in the back seat of his car, Richard drove me to Wright County. We got down there in the later part of the afternoon and I noted that the town was filled with cars with hardly even a parking place available.

I commented to Richard that there must be something important going on and Richard said, "They said that they would do a good job getting people out."

It still hadn't dawned on me that they had come to hear *me*, and when I finally came to that realization, I was real shook up. I was introduced to the head of the meeting, who had apparently done a lot of work to notify all these people. There was a full high school auditorium and at least a couple of dozen priests. I learned that this area was pretty much Catholic and that the head of the meeting was a CEO or President of the Saint Thomas College in the cities. It had been announced in their parish that I would be speaking this evening. I asked if the record books were available in case some should choose to pay some of their dues after hearing my presentation this evening.

"Yes," they said, "they were."

Well, I really wished I'd had some time to devote to preparation. I saw that they had a few books on a card table and thought those were the records which could be referred to. As I recall, the appointed hour was eight o'clock in the evening because these people had their chores and milking to do before coming to the meeting. They opened with a prayer and a few formalities, after which I was introduced.

I was literally shaking in my boots. I think I gave a good history of the NFO and related just what it was that we were trying to do. I must have related something that they approved of because they gave me a number of standing ovations, which gave me confidence and helped me to understand just what they wanted to hear. You could hear a pin drop while I was speaking and I noted that I had a very attentive audience. After speaking for over an hour, I started to wrap it up when I received another standing ovation along with thunderous applause.

They were serving lunch afterward and the college president asked if I would allow him to visit with me.

I said, "Yes," and wondered if my speaking had been all right.

I had noted before my speech that there was a card table and some books and now observed there was a lot of people in line. I mentioned that maybe a couple more tables were in order and the president sent some priests to set up more tables. Would you believe that before everyone had paid what they could, about seven lines had formed across the auditorium? Many people were congratulating me on the interesting speech.

Then came the "shock of the evening" when the president asked me if he could hire me to teach at St. Thomas!

I said, "What would I teach?"

He said, "Homiletics."

I asked, "What it that?"

He replied, "Homiletics is the art of putting something across, and you certainly accomplished that here tonight!"

I said, You can't be serious—do you realize that you are talking to a high school drop-out?"

He answered, "Mr. Ekberg, I have never witnessed anything like this in my life. I am dead serious!"

Well, I had a lot to do at home so I thanked the president and said, "Good-bye."

The "Get Us Together Address"

I have been so very concerned that the "Get Us Together Address" be understood. After much hassling and thinking, this address does seem unusual—at least to me. I want to make a special effort to explain this to you, the reader, and to bring to your attention the meaning of the word *harbinger*, which is a warning from God and shows something is coming.

All my life I had at times noted things I thought should not be done, and things that were not being done that should be! The things that come to my mind were both big and little. Do I sound like a rather arrogant and bigoted individual? Really, I do hope that is not the case!

For example, I was amazed to learn when I was 15 years old that agricultural sprayers were used to control weeds when the crops first came up. I thought that the sprays that killed wild mustard, thistle, pigweed and other unwanted weeds were terrific because they spared the agricultural plants, such as wheat, other grains and corn. It was a good thing, as I for one did not enjoy picking wild mustard and the like.

But I really had my doubts when the chemical companies started altering agricultural seed genes so that every living plant would be killed except the crop seed that was planted, as in the case of Round Up®. But it had neonics, which were harmful to bees!! (I had nine hives of bees when I was a teenager. I really got to like and enjoy honeybees. My first presentation about bees occurred when I was 12 years old. In later years, I started making presentations on bees and wildlife to students at area schools.) The sprays were the things that made me resent chemicals so much and then it seemed some areas had a lot of cancer, for which chemicals were now suspect.

Well, it was the agricultural herbal sprays that prompted me to promote the Lawndale Environmental Foundation (LEF). Three area businessmen who were friends of mine helped me to organize the LEF: Leonard Blume (the John Deere machinery dealer in Herman), Robert Anderson (Superintendent of schools at Herman), and Melvyn W. Townsend of Fergus Falls (a concessionaire of foot-long hot dogs and a great conservationist). These three formed the nucleus, while several area Odd Fellow friends and a number of wildlife artists made up a fine group of environmentalists and gave us a good start. At this site at the foundation, we have sponsored several programs, which were lined up by my wife. The Board arranged earlier major events.

In one of our first discussions, the outcome was that I should write down the purpose of LEF. There were no special instructions, except that it was to be environmental in nature and honor God! So, with that brief, but significant comment, I for days ran this over in my mind and nothing seemed to fit. I know that I repeatedly prayed for direction and nothing ... then one morning in November 1990 I awoke at a little after two o'clock in the morning. I still had not received direction, but went out in the kitchen to see if there might be a "bite" to eat.

I had a couple of sheets of paper with me, but no ideas about what to write. I thought maybe I should start out with a poem or some well-known quotation and see if anything came to me—maybe I could go on from there! Then I was running over in my mind the Gettysburg Address—"Fourscore and seven years ago..." was the start of that splendid piece of oratory and it seemed right! The only problem was I only had a couple of lines that seemed to fit; I had never memorized the entire poem—something always came up so I only knew the few first words, that was all I was sure about. But it did seem that the cadence would fit right in. I looked around the house for a copy of the Gettysburg Address and found nothing. I decided right there to utilize words that would fit.

Well, I worked at the kitchen table for about an hour, more or less, and never changed a word. The paper was going together pretty well, which was somewhat different from when I had done writing before. It seemed strange that it had come together so quickly. I read it over a couple times and it sounded good to me. I essentially had written it in about an hour's time and had not changed anything once I had written it down. Then I thought I had better think up a title, and "Get Us Together Address" seemed to fit right in!

I got up later that morning about 8 o'clock and read it a couple times. It still seemed "right." I wanted to take it in for the editor of our weekly newspaper to comment on. Why did I do that? Because I was quite sure that I had done a good job and it had taken such a short time. I asked the editor, Owen Heiberg, to give me his opinion. I was watching his face as he leisurely took the paper and started to read. I could see his eyes light up as he was reading and upon reaching the end he excitedly exclaimed, "Good Lord, Gordon, this is inspired!"

I had no idea what that exclamation meant.

He said that a force beyond ourselves had taken ahold of me and conveyed the words to me! God could have been instrumental in what I wrote.

I was shocked, but I did know that it was something that I had never had happen before. That promulgated an effort to see if that might be the case. I could hardly believe it, until after I had read the address in a live broadcast at a Fargo-Moorhead television station. They had assembled background visual and sound enhancements. After this presentation "aired," we started getting letters from all over our area from many, many people who expressed Owen's evaluation and wondered if they could get a copy. And some just liked the writing. There were letters from people I knew and from people I had never heard of—a college CEO, theologians, ministers, school teachers, farmers and businessmen! I was amazed at the response, and I started to believe Owen was right.

One of the most interesting comments was expressed visually by a close personal friend, popular political cartoonist Delmar (Del) Holdgrafer of Donnelly, Minnesota. Del stopped in quite often. One day he walked into our gallery and there was no one around. The rather scribbled "Get Us Together Address" was on the counter, so Del read it over. He was so impressed that he took a copy home and drew a border for it, which enhanced the writing very much. What an illustration! The next day he came back and we talked about the writing. Del said, "You know what you wrote is special, you must publicize it." It was after this that I read it over Fargo-Moorhead television station.

I had felt that maybe it would be a good idea to paraphrase what I had written so I could be sure everyone got the right meaning, so here it goes:

The Get Us Together Address, paraphrased version:

It had always seemed to me that so often we were not United in our efforts, some of the things that we did or did not do I thought were so obvious that everyone would understand. For example, Stop the Pebble Mine in Alaska, Do NOT Spray the Bees, Do NOT Destroy the Birds, Save the Butterflies. I thought this to be common sense.

Original writing for "Get Us Together Address":

Thousands of years ago, Our Father brought forth upon this planet a new creation, conceived in love, and dedicated to the proposition that all things are related. We are now engaged in a great environmental battle, testing whether this planet or any component of it, so conceived and so dedicated can long endure.

Paraphrase:

Our Father and our God, so says the Bible, created this beautiful well-thought-out dwelling for us to live and move and have our being, to recognize each other as alike, the offspring of the same parent, as the master piece of his handiwork to reflect in our nature and relation to the image of Him. Man was formed, we were therefore charged with living and working as though whatever we did would have an effect on all those things, whether plant or animal, that were involved. The Native American Indian conveyed this knowledge quite simply and fairly accurately by referring to the various animals with which they had contact. As Brother Bear, Brother Beaver, Brother Buffalo, etc., so that we were more apt to understand that what we did was not of a regular consequence but did affect others in many different ways. Not only plants, animals, birds, and creatures of the sea, but the water and the very air that we breathe. All are affected in varying degrees! And the sooner we understand this the better it will be for all of creation!

The actual Address:

We are met on this great battlefield of that war, our environment. We have come to dedicate a portion of our lives toward a sustaining dwelling place for all creatures and to a comprehension of love and relationship to all things and all people, that this planet might live. It is altogether fitting and proper and essential that we do this, but in a larger sense ... We can not dedicate, we can not hallow, we can not consecrate this Earth, for the Great God that created it ... perceived it ... and conceived it ... far beyond our poor power to add or detract.

Paraphrase follows:

We have come here together on this Earth, the rich and the poor, the high and the low, the educated and the ignorant, not as comes of the Earth, but as bearers of each others' burdens. There is no doubt that we can do this, if we want to! And we MUST want to cooperate, if we want this planet to live.

The Address continues:

The World will little note nor long remember what we say, but it can not ignore and will never forget what we do here.

Paraphrase follows:

Talk is cheap, commitment is what we really need! They were men of their word.

The Address continues:

It is now for us, the living, to take up the task as laid out by God and expounded on by men such as Thoreau, Muir, and Leopold ... and project the theories they so nobly advanced.

Paraphrased:

It places the responsibility right on the inhabitants of the planet, the earth! Is it a warning from God, a harbinger as the Hebrew language would label it? It is like nothing else that has ever happened to me before!!!

The Address continues:

It is rather for all of us to be here dedicated to the great task remaining before us ... that we take increased devotion to the cause of cultivating the understanding of the integral and imperative relationship that exists between man and nature and all things in nature ... that we here highly resolve that this planet, under God, shall have a new birth of environmental stewardship ... and that responsible and dedicated stewardship of the air, of the water, of the land and of all creatures ... shall not perish from the Earth.

Believe It or Not, Ripley

Here are some interesting local facts that Robert Ripley considered interesting enough for his column.

At one time, the largest railroad gravel pit in the world was owned by the Great Northern and was located between Elbow Lake and Erdahl. It also spawned a village known as West Elbow Lake.

Barrett has a cemetery located just north of town that has an operating airplane propeller on a tombstone!

The area has the shortest United States highway that begins and ends in Grant County without touching any town. Highway 54 is 11 miles long, was paved in 1953, and runs from Elbow Lake's south edge down to Highway 27, providing a link from Herman to the county seat.

Not in Ripley's but equally fascinating was when local well drillers brought up a prehistoric fish, almost opaque in color and blind because of no exposure to light. Taken to the Barrett High School for inspection, it was inadvertently flushed down a toilet. It was quite the find, nonetheless!

Gordon and his ferret, Mickey (1942)
Grandpa Ekberg had given him an extra $5.00 so that he could buy a pair!

Ferrets

Hunting Rats, Cottontails and Mink

The name and address of Levi Farnsworth, Rte-B1, New London, Ohio, has stuck in my mind since around 1940. Why? Well, this is the man from whom I had purchased a pair of ferrets those many years ago. I had really enjoyed many hours of great fun with my interest in ferrets during my later boyhood years. So because of the great fun and hunting experiences I had those many years ago, I thought it would be interesting to see if there were any relatives still living in the area of the address that was so firmly etched on my memory. I had a friend who is an expert on locating people on the Internet. I called the number I was given, but was not successful. The person who answered said that in their area in Ohio those people passed away, others who bought the property for some reason did not have their name transferred as the new owner. Anyway, I did have a nice phone conversation with the person now living on the Farnsworth property, who was most congenial.

Well, back to the 1940s when I had purchased the ferrets. As you may possibly know a ferret is a member of the weasel/mink family and is used to being sent down the hole of other animals to drive them out. I had several choices to make.

For instance, I could choose the English Ferret, which had a white coat of fur and had pink eyes and was more aggressive. Or I could choose the Fitch Ferret, which had brown fur and black eyes with little colored rings of fur on its face that made it look like a raccoon, and was also more docile.

There was also the choice of small, medium or large. It was said the large ferrets would drive a fox from its den.

I chose a small-sized pair of Fitch—being smaller, they would have easier access to the burrow of the Gray Norway Rat, which I had chosen to pursue. I had the ferrets for a number of years, and chased rats for fun and for hire. There was really a kind of science to chasing rats. I learned it was necessary to be aware when releasing the ferrets that the rats had three levels within their living quarters. The first level, a kind of pathway, was for easy and rapid movement in the area. The second level was a few inches under the first level and was a little more secure and somewhat more developed for living quarters. The third level was the deepest and the most secure—it was the safest living quarters and used for storage of food.

When I came on a property, I had to give the ferrets plenty of time to pursue the rats and be patient as they patrolled all levels of the complex—the rats migrated to the lowest level and did not want to come out where people with clubs or dogs could get them. So you see, the rats kept going deeper and would avoid a tunnel only after a ferret had gone though it leaving its scent behind. The ferrets had a big job to patrol all three levels of the complex until finally the ferret scent became evident throughout the rat complex. Only then would the rats make their escape to the outside world to the dogs and clubs.

I used ferrets on cottontail rabbits and mink also, but was most successful with hunting rats—once driven out, it was generally some time before the rats would inhabit the area again.

I also raised ferrets for a number of years, and that was fun too.

Running in Circles

No, Crossing the Arctic Circle

All my life I had wanted to go to Alaska. Why not Norway? They were both up North! I did not have many relatives in Alaska, but many relatives in Norway! Just what was so enticing about Alaska? I suppose it was the frontier and the native Eskimos—the native unsettledness seemed more beckoning than the more settled homeland of my relatives. I suppose Norway and Alaska both had wild game of both bird and animal species—so there were many similarities, and yet Alaska won out! And then I was applying for egg-collecting permits for a variety of waterfowl species—since Alaska was a part of the United States, it seemed easier to apply in my country! Then, of course, we had studied a lot more about the U.S. in school.

First Trip:

And so it was. I went to Alaska in January 1981, because I thought one of the species I was interested in, the spectacled eiders (sea ducks about 20 inches in length with a green head, bright orange bill and white "spectacles" around the eyes), would congregate in certain areas at that time of the year, but that did not work out. I learned that it is far better to find the nests in the spring season—at least the eggs won't walk away!

The natural scenic area along Alaska's Arctic coast where the ducks nest is breathtaking. It was a rather expensive trip, but what beautiful country—I was literally mesmerized with its beauty. This nesting trip yielded 67 or 68 eggs, with some hatching on the way home. We had no reason to cross the Arctic Circle on this trip.

The mystery of the migration of the spectacled eider was finally solved about ten years ago. For many years, American and Asian biologists had been mystified: where did the beautiful spectacled eiders migrate for the winter? No matter how clever the surveillance, the major portion of the breeding flock always eluded the watchful eyes of the biologists. What a mystery!

The specialized surveillance planes (small, fuel-efficient spotting planes) always lost the huge migrating birds somewhere along the anticipated southerly route. Then one day about ten years ago, a spotting plane got lost in a fog and drifted much too far north from the supposed migration route, and lo and behold, spectacled eiders started showing up. Instead of going south—the direction most other species migrate—the spectacled eiders migrate to the north, of all things!

It seems the entire global population of spectacled eiders winter in gaps in the sea ice in the Bering Sea between St. Lawrence and St. Matthew Islands. They use these gaps in the ice to dive down and collect mollusks and other crustaceans from the sea floor. With the entire breeding flock constantly diving deep, the huge area stays open. God has some wonderful secrets that protect His charges!

Nearly 170 years ago the big attraction in Alaska was the discovery of gold. While the mining of minerals and gold is still important, the oil reserves hold a major attraction today. However, what attracted my attention (and the reason I went to Alaska), was the opportunity to collect wild waterfowl eggs to enhance my collection of wild waterfowl!

Now collecting eggs was not like going to a store and choosing merchandise. We had to have permits for the various species before we went. We needed three different permits for each species we intended to collect—even if we might never encounter them out on the tundra. To be prepared, we did have our pockets full of permits!

Collecting eggs on the tundra worked like this. Two people walked closely together across the tundra, focusing on the terrain ahead as we scanned for nesting waterfowl. A bird, duck or goose would sense us coming and stick its head up for only a few seconds before it pulled its head quickly back down—and we might never see it again! So, one of us stood still with his eyes "glued" to the spot and directed the other person to the nest. This worked well and was great fun! We collected a number of eggs in this manner. But we had to watch our step and be aware of just where we were going because there were bears out on the tundra—and they really didn't care for company.

In fact, we were warned about that when we departed from the plane in Kodiak Island. How? There was a museum at Kodiak Island that specialized in showing mounted specimens of Kodiak bears at the airport. One does not soon forget the various poses of the bears displayed—especially those that are mounted standing on their two back legs! How high from the ground to the top of their heads? Would you believe nine feet? We really did not want to blunder into one of them while innocently collecting duck eggs out on the tundra! Also, a moose doesn't have much more of a "welcome mat" out than does a Kodiak bear, so we were encouraged to watch out! The great outdoors in Alaska is so disarmingly beautiful—if we didn't pay attention, we could be welcomed by a most unwelcome bear hug!

I was also looking forward to eating seal and walrus. Well, the seal we had for supper tasted like a billy goat smells! Enough said. One of the other interesting things in Alaska is that in some places the tide varied as much as 12 feet! And the seafood—what a delightful event to get our fill of Alaska King Crab! Would you believe I left about 20 pounds of dressed King Crab sitting on the dock when I left Alaska? I regretted leaving behind this gift from our hosts.

Another delicious food was butter clams. We waited for the tide to go out, then drove the truck near the ocean's edge and dug butter clams that had been covered by 12 feet of sea water only an hour before we dug them! If you ever go to Alaska, you'll always want to go back!

Second Trip:
And go back I did! We were fortunate enough to get a second opportunity and permits to return to Alaska on June 17-26, 1981. This time we went

to St. Lawrence Island and crossed over the Arctic Circle on our way to Kotzebue on June 24. "We never dreamed we'd get two permits from Alaska again this year, but we did, so we will go. You have to make hay while the sun shines" (Gordon quoted in *Fergus Falls Daily Journal*, 7/2/81).

Referring to the first trip to Kodiak Island in January, Kathy Berdan from the *Fergus Falls Daily Journal* (7/2/81), wrote:

> *The waterfowl project has driven the soft-spoken farmer to activities such as lashing himself to the side of a boat in the dark Arctic night armed with a flashlight. Ekberg and some companions traveled to Kodiak Islands to capture Arctic waterfowl and collect eggs.*

> *The flashlight beams that sliced through the chilly darkness attracted the ducks ... a bit like shining deer and Ekberg's group got a special governmental permit to experiment with the flashlight lure. The group brought back 70 eggs at various stages of development from Alaska. Ekberg and another waterfowl enthusiast were able to hatch 68 of those fragile structures.*

> *There were only 12 permits for duck gathering in Alaska issued in the whole world last year ... Two of these permits went with the Ekberg party. This trip will not involve duck collecting. The group plans to restrict itself to gathering fertile eggs ... to a remote area known for its spring migration.*

Referring to this second trip, the *Journal* article stated:

> *Gordon said that he saw snow-capped mountains of Siberia from the western-most edge of the (St. Lawrence) island. The island is just 20 miles from the International Date Line ... If you were on the western edge of St. Lawrence Island right now reading this today, Thursday, you would*

be just twenty miles from Friday. Gordon called the island
"desolate." No trees, not even low bushes. But it does have
its beauty ... the tundra is alive with flowers, beautiful
flowers, delicate flowers. And the tundra is loaded with
nests ... common (Pacific) eider, king eider, Pacific black
Brant, great scaup, Steller's eider—and other eggs—
emperor geese, whistling swans, sandhill cranes. Gordon
and the others brought some of each of those kinds of eggs
back with them.

They saw whales ... "We almost ran into two in the fog
when we were out in the boat. There were whale skeletons
washed up on the beach, too. That is when I realized how
large whales actually are. Just massive. The economy is
ivory. The Eskimos are tremendous artists, carving figures
out of the tusks of walrus." Gordon brought some small
ivory carvings back with him as well as vertebrae disks
from whales—about the size of dinner plates.

While I was getting on the flight in Anchorage, a couple from
Morris thought they spotted me with my big black cowboy hat. Some
of the whistling swans were hatching in flight, so at the Seattle airport
I spread newspaper on the men's restroom floor and sprinkled some
feed for the cygnets. Mr. Day walked in and exclaimed, "Gordon Ekberg,
what are you doing? We thought we recognized you getting on the plane
in Anchorage!" It is a small world! The remainder of the eggs were
eventually taken to an incubator in my basement.

The two whistling swans ... are outside in the small
building where Gordon's ducks and geese spend the
winter. The three cranes—tall, tan, gangly chicks—are in
cardboard boxes ... I have to keep them in separate boxes
or they will kill each other. (Gordon quoted in Fergus
Falls Daily Journal.)

Gordon with a King Crab on Kodiak Island, Alaska

Michael Loss (Brainerd) along with Dennis Alberts and his son Curtis Alberts on the St. Lawrence Island in Alaska. While looking for waterfowl eggs on the tundra, Gordon took their picture on this bullet-riddled jet that had crash-landed a long time ago, probably during the World War II era. The electronics had been taken out.
This was Gordon's second trip to Alaska, July 1981, and he saw Gamble and other villages. They also found a human skull by a fox trap – a bit unnerving.
Gordon took a "net gun," a new invention to shoot a rubber torpedo leading a full net system to fly out and surround the designated waterfowl. Unfortunately, it arrived a day before leaving for Alaska and allowed no time to "practice" this tool.

I Know These Guys!

DAVID MCIVER

If you have an opportunity to access the June/July 2016 issue of *Mother Earth News*, you may find the article on page 51 of interest to you. I think you might find some of the farming methods of David McIver from Farwell, Minnesota, most interesting! These methods that Mr. McIver has subscribed to for approximately 40 years are free of chemicals, being good for the soil, his livestock, crops and gardens. It is amazing what great results he has to show and demonstrate! (Read more about his methods in the chapter *Agriculture and the Environment*.)

JAMES SARGENT LOMBARD

It is not hard to write about someone that I liked as well as knew: Jim Lombard. My association with Jim was primarily through the Independent Order of Odd Fellows (IOOF). We were personal friends as well as fraternal friends! I was an overnight guest at his home on more than one occasion, so we could get an early morning start on lengthy trips to an Odd Fellow event destination. I had also had the honor of being chosen by Jim through H. Sanders Anglea of Nashville, Tennessee, to make the nominating speech at a Sovereign Grand Lodge (SGL) session in Chicago, Illinois. You see, Jim had chosen to run for Sovereign Grand Warden, which ultimately put him in full charge of the what is now the Educational Pilgrimage for Youth. However, we failed to get Jim nominated for Sovereign Grand Warden and I often wonder what would have happed if Jim had won. I do know that Jim's election, if successful, would have been carried by most major newspapers in the country. You see, Jim was instrumental in helping to make St. Paul/ Minneapolis, Minnesota, the center of culture and art in the mid-western United States! Jim had a unique connection with our town and lodge of Herman's Harmony Lodge #30—Ernest E. Peck, President of the First National Bank of Herman, chose Jim as one of his staff officers when he became Grand Master of the Odd Fellows of Minnesota in 1928. If I remember right, Jim was on the road to becoming the youngest Grand Master of the Odd Fellows under the Sovereign Grand Lodge.

That sounds like politics, but it was also ability! As a young man, Jim was employed by the Standard Oil Company. He put so much effort into the Odd Fellows that he lost his job with Standard Oil. Jim then took the schooling that allowed him to become a minister of a Presbyterian Church in the Chicago, Illinois, area. I joined the IOOF on January 28, 1948, when Jim was Grand Patriarch of the Grand Encampment of Minnesota. He was also serving in Odd Fellow and Rebekah youth work. It was my privilege to assist Jim on committees and it was amazing to see things happen on any project with Jim at the helm! He accepted a committee assignment with the SGL and was able to put together what is now known as the Educational Pilgrimage for Youth, which turned out to be the most outstanding young people's educational tour in the United States.

His official title was Director of the Department of Concerts and Lectures of the University of Minnesota, Northrup Auditorium. One of Jim's stipulations was that any committee that he was on would consist of himself as chairman and one other person. Such a request was most unusual, but legal—a way to surely get things done!

Jim's death was duly noted in most area news. I and one other Odd Fellow, a member of Flour City Lodge #118, conducted the Odd Fellow rites the evening before the funeral. I was chaplain and the other brother acted as Noble Grand. I was honored to be asked to be one of the pall bearers.

After the evening Odd Fellow Rites, an announcement was made for all pall bearers to be punctual at 1 p.m. at the Waylander Quist mortuary the following day for the funeral. I was shocked that I, along with all the physically-able past Governors of Minnesota, had been asked to be pall bearers. The mortuary was filling rapidly as I was ushered to a seat about 2/3 midway up the mortuary auditorium. There were a few seats open around me. At the time indicated for the start of the service, I noted what seemed to be a certain amount of commotion in my area, and I gathered that a person of significant public stature was being seated next to me. I looked straight ahead and didn't look at him, but I stole a sideways glance without moving my head—seated next to me was the Honorable Hubert Humphrey, the Vice President of the United States! He was officially present to honor Jim. I almost fell out of my chair!

MELVYN WARREN TOWNSEND

In the late 1800s, a family named Blake moved in north of us and had a profound influence on our lives. Not so much directly, but rather indirectly, as it was through Emmet Eldon Blake's wife that we met and became friends of Muggs Townsend, aka Melvyn Warren Townsend. Florence Blake was Muggs' first cousin. The entire Blake family, and that includes Blakes, Townsends, and Champlins, was most interesting and capable. Muggs never got his college degree. He wanted to show that he did not need a college degree to be a success in life. Oh, Muggs went through most all of his college classes, stopping short of accepting his diploma. Muggs was known as a "master of impulse sales."

During the year I went on the road with Muggs, he gave me a series of lectures on how to sell his famous footlong hot dogs and caramel apples at fairs and events in the Midwest. They were so interesting that I don't believe I have ever forgotten any of them. One time, Muggs and I were finishing up some last-minute details in our respective homes prior to leaving for the Tulip Festival at Orange City, Iowa. It was my first experience in selling, and I just thought that we went ahead and sold.

Please let me explain. We got down to Orange City after a late start and all the good sites were taken around the Village Square, so I said to Muggs, "Where will we set up our stands?" The other vendors were all set up around the Square, leaving no room for us. The only open spot was by a group of trees in the park by a lake. We squeezed in a 12-foot by 5-foot spot for the footlong hot dogs complemented by a Coke Flucom machine to dispense glasses of Coca- Cola®. People were going by our stand without buying either hot dogs or Cokes. Muggs said:

> We have to use our heads when the people go by our stand. Smile and pleasantly invite them to buy hot dogs and Coke! When the public goes by us down to the stands, no one is hungry, and when they come back they have visited other stands and in many cases, eaten their full. Now, we have to utilize sales psychology!

> Visualize a young couple, a boy and a girl, coming toward us going home. They may or may not have eaten our footlong hot dogs and Coke. Using our most cordial manners and smile we invite them to do so. Now is when the sales psychology comes in. It is most crucial at what time you speak and issue the cordial smile and invitation. The young man must have plenty of time when first hearing your voice to be able to reach into his pocket, get his hand on his billfold, extract an adequate sum of money and be right exactly in front of you. Issue the invitation too soon or too late so that the couple is not quite up to you or has gone a foot or so past you, you have lost the sale. Do it exactly right, and nine times out of ten you will have made the sale.

The same thing applies when selling in a grandstand—be sure to issue the invitation to buy **before** you walk up a few steps, which most inexperienced vendors don't do. Take note that by waiting to issue the invitation to buy after walking up a few rows, you have already eliminated the invitation to the ground and first, second, third, and whatever rows you have passed before speaking. It is little things like that which make the difference between a salesman and a super-salesman—it doesn't seem like much, but it does make a difference in the day's receipts at the end of the day.

Muggs was also a great wildlife conservationist. He was a major factor in the establishment in the "Save the Wetlands Club" of Fergus Falls.

Selling foot long hot dogs "on the road" with Muggs Townsend

Muggs Townsend visiting with Gordon and Gay in their kitchen

Camping
From Mustinka River to
Yumperhaugen Hill

I've "camped out" from the Florida Keys when attending a meeting in southern Florida, to the North Pole (well, almost!) while gathering eggs in Alaska. Here are some of the camping stories in between!

Nearly all boys, and a lot of girls, seem to have an innate desire to go camping. At least it seems to come naturally. I think my first effort at camping—putting up a semblance of a shelter and sleeping in it overnight—involved putting up an old card table behind the house and draping an extra-large blanket over it. Of course, my feet stuck out and mosquitoes came in, leaving a lot to be desired, but it was fun!

It was not long before the anticipated attempt at imitating pioneer living happened. My first camping trip was with my buddy Ray Danzeisen when I was about 12 years old. We made the journey on our ponies to a spot a couple of miles straight north of home near the Mustinka River. There was no thought of even setting up a crude imitation of a tent on that trip. Our camping instincts were fueled by the thought of gourmet food. We feasted on roasted frog legs, as only two 12-year-old kids could make them.

It was early in the spring—the frogs were awakening from their over-winter hibernation and were easy "game" to catch. We built a little campfire as we skinned and dressed the frog legs, which we roasted like marshmallows on a green willow stick until they were golden brown, adding a few crystals of salt. Those frog legs sure were good, which Ray and I still attest to some 50 years after the fact! That was not a very long trip nor did it last long, but it was a most memorable trip and our first camping adventure!

Then it was a couple of years before I took a week-long vacation and rented a cabin on Lake Minnewaska at Starbuck with my neighborhood friends: Bill Marth, Gene Kreidler, Neil Kreidler, Milton Lueneburg and Donald Johnson.

A couple of years later, I put up a tent on Yumperhaugen Hill on Barrett Lake with Roger and Wallace Andersen and my dog Spot. I mention Spot because he got tired of camping about the second or third night and trotted along home in the early morning hours, scaring my father half to death for fear something had happened to us boys!

Then it was a few years before my mother's friends, the Blakes, invited me to come up to their place near Pelican Rapids, about 70 miles north of our place, for a few days of deer hunting. I invited my good friend, Bob Richards, to accompany me—that was a fun time and a successful trip.

That trip inspired the two of us, along with a few more friends from the Odd Fellow Lodge in Herman and Muggs Townsend from Fergus Falls, into organizing an annual deer hunt—which I enjoyed for many years until old age interfered. One highlight of those hunting trips was making homemade sherbet with our family recipe from the 1800s. Another was the retelling and reciting of the poem *Sam McGee*.

I also organized and planned three trips to the Boundary Water Canoe Area located up at Ely, Minnesota. I can't remember who went on which trip, but I do remember some of the rather humorous events that took place! The prize for eating the most pancakes at one sitting went to Mike Ogg, who downed 21 six-inch-diameter pancakes. The pancakes weren't so good—it was just that everybody got so overly hungry before we got to the campsite, where we had to get the tents set up before dark. Then on at least one of the trips we were deluged with rainstorms. Mike Nelson and his friend by the last name of Sanford saved the day by volunteering to go on ahead on a well-marked trail to the campsite to get at least one tent set up and a camp stove going so we could have warm soup when the rest of us got there.

If you have never been to the Wilderness Canoe country, you have certainly missed out on some of God's most beautiful creation! More than once a bear announced its presence and thrilled us all!

On one trip, the group went through an elaborate effort to stage a waterskiing event—behind a canoe! It worked like this: in an area where there were a number of submerged boulders, one of the guys stood on a very large and stable rock, while the rest of the guys took about a 15-foot-long rope and held it in the canoe. Well, it looked for all the world like this one guy was being pulled by a half dozen guys in the lead canoe. It sure looked like the real thing! This stunt got a lot of publicity, as it looked like they were going fast enough that the skier was being pulled by the canoe! Ha!

Gordon and crew of area boys he took to the Boundary Waters Canoe Area for a week of portaging and camping in 1971

That year Gordon also grew a beard for the Herman Centennial and won the contest. Being a bachelor, he turned down the prize – a weekend for two in the Twin Cities.

*Gordon and buddies
Wally and Roger
Andersen back from
duck hunting*

*This was also the day
that Gordon's beloved
dog Spot disappeared.*

*Gordon at deer camp with sons John and Joel. John began going to camp in 2ⁿᵈ grade.
back, l-r: Eldon Blake (a friend and eldest hunter in camp), Gordon, Joel
front: John*

Stories the Old-Timers Tell

Years ago, I got to wondering if my aunts and uncles, parents and even grandparents got into things they weren't supposed to, especially at times when their parents either went to town, went visiting or otherwise left the place. When I asked my Aunt Effie, she replied that, yes, they certainly did. She was in her 50s at the time, and did not mind relating stories of "yesteryear" regardless of how hair-raising they might be.

The first story she told was about herself, and pretty much seemed to bear out the fact that kids were concerned about their home life and whether it was even a little bit different from the neighbors, such as a family member having a small birthmark on their face.

In the case of my Aunt Effie, she was most self-conscious about being the only girl in a family of four boys. What she did about it was something only an eight-year-old girl could dream up! She tried her best to make strangers who came on the place think that there were a number of girls in the family. How did she do it? Well, her father was somewhat of a horse trader and consequently had a number of people coming on the place to view horses, and he often invited them into the house for a social cup of coffee and maybe a donut or two.

Now, the house was built so that the outside door opened into the kitchen where the horse-trading guests were being seated. The kitchen had an archway that opened onto the dining room, which had a door leading into a bedroom. This door opened quite easily. The bedroom, for some reason or another, had about three or four footstools of varying heights. The charade of portraying the presence of several girls in the family was accomplished by having the guests seated in such a manner around the kitchen table so the guests could see the bedroom door, which was cracked open wide enough for Aunt Effie to stick her face out at various heights. The guests could see what was going on, but my grandfather was seated so that he could not. The guests were treated to a big toothy smile or various other facial contortions by my aunt as she stood on the different footstools. This charade caused the guests to think that girls of different ages were looking at them! My grandfather with his back to the inner door was totally unaware of this silly charade, which was the talk of the neighborhood for several months!

Another stunt was accomplished by my aunt, her older brother and some neighbor kids on the way home from school. This group of a half dozen kids were starting small prairie fires on the way home from school. They would allow the fires to get into a full blaze, and then snuff them out by pounding on them with their jackets. It appears the goal was to see how big they could allow the fire to get before safely putting it out, certainly an ill-advised and dangerous goal.

As you might have guessed, on one day the worst happened: an unexpected sharp, strong breeze escalated the little fire into the roaring inferno of a major uncontrolled prairie fire! All efforts to snuff out the blaze failed and my uncle Oscar ran home for his dad. Other family members were dispatched to notify neighbors to bring plows and horses to plow a furrow in the prairie. After hours of intense effort, the flames were finally brought under control. The parents administered the punishment to their respective kids, and that was the last of playing "Prairie Fire."

And now for a look at one of the most dangerous child escapades I have ever heard of! My grandfather had purchased a revolver, a .38 Smith and Wesson, which was totally off limits to the five children who had been told that *under no circumstances* were they ever to touch nor go near this revolver. What happened? One time, when the oldest boy was a teenager and the others were a couple of years younger and the kids were home alone, they decided to practice marksmanship with the revolver.

What to use for a target? It was decided to put a bulls-eye target on the door of the outhouse and have fun target practicing. That might have been all well and good, except that they couldn't readily see where the bullets were going. What to do.

My Aunt Effie, who at that time was a pre-teenager, was talked into going into the outhouse to announce just where the bullets came through. Yes, that worked. She would open the outhouse door and announce just where the deadly muster of bullets were coming through.

"There is one! Up there! There is one down lower!" she exclaimed.

Why she was never hit had to be by the grace of God! The kids never told this episode to the parents until many years later, and even then the parents grew weak with the thought of what could have happened. A true story, vividly remembered and related to me by my Aunt Effie. Oh, yes, the kids got into mischief back then, too!

Frank and Augusta Ekberg family: children Irven, Effie, Walter, Oscar and Ray (front)

The Sheep Enterprise

When we sold the cattle, I was what you would call "lost." After having up to 36 milk cows and my dad's feeder cattle, the place seemed empty.

Well, that did not last very long. I started to think about having sheep—we had some good pastures, and it seemed a shame to plow them up after some very real effort had been expended to get some good stands of "bloat-free" pastures for the cattle. Raising sheep would fit right into that situation.

But "the other side of the coin" was that my father did not like sheep, and he lived on this place, too! My grandfather, Frank A. Ekberg, had been talked into getting some purebred Shropshire sheep by none other than James J. Hill, the "Empire Builder", but after a few years my grandfather did not care about them and sold them. Since his folks did not care for the sheep, it influenced my father's opinion as well—so much so that he did not want them on the place. So I just kind of gave up the idea.

Then one day my father had been visiting one of his good friends, Albert Kietzman, who inquired how it was not to have cattle. And unbeknownst to me, my father was really missing the cattle! Well, Mr. Kietzman gave my dad an argument about how much a flock of sheep would remedy that! And by chance he, Mr. Kietzman, was getting to the age where he wanted to cut down and sell his sheep and would offer me, Gordon, a good deal!

Dad came home from Kietzman's and suggested that I go and see what the "good deal" was. I couldn't believe my ears that Dad was suggesting that I go and talk to Mr. Kietzman about sheep!

Don't worry! I did not waste any time! First of all, I went to see what was up and to see if I could borrow the money to buy Albert Kietzman's sheep. Yes, indeed, the bank would loan me the money if the deal was attractive enough. Then I went over to Albert Kietzman's to see what the deal was.

It turned out that there were 32 bred ewes (female sheep) and a ram (a male sheep). The sheep were pretty much white-faced wool producers such as Columbia and Rambouillet. The ewes were to start giving birth to lambs in January, and with our barns empty, Mr. Kietzman said that should work out very well. Because the sheep would be giving birth in January, the rather tender newborn lambs had to have protection from the cold weather.

I was advised to be sure and shear the sheep prior to their giving birth to their lambs. The two reasons for doing so were: 1) the body heat from the adult sheep would tend to warm the barn for an overall benefit, and 2) the newborn lamb would find difficulty in nursing the mother's teat by mistaking a tuft of wool for the teat and thus get no nourishment for its efforts in sucking on a tuft of wool. This was a common mistake, particularly among the long wool varieties.

Mr. Kietzman also gave me a good bargain on sheep equipment such as hay feeders and lambing pens. And so I bought the sheep, all 32 ewes and the ram.

That first year I rented our neighbor Louis Reuss's barn, which was only about a quarter of a mile away and was standing empty. I thought that, considering my father's feeling about sheep, it was the best course of action.

Then I got the best advice I could from other people who raised sheep. One of the first things to do appeared to get them sheared so that their body heat would warm up the barn. When I eventually got the whole flock of sheep sheared, there was a remarkable warming effect that made the barn nice and cozy. But first, how to get the shearing done?

I thought that I could do that myself as I had for years clipped my dairy herd and shearing sheep must be a similar operation. By doing it myself, I could save the money it would cost to hire someone else to shear the sheep. Right?

Well, let me tell you that the "art" of shearing sheep is indeed an art, and a highly-skilled art that is not learned in a few days. My good friend Bob Richards offered me the opportunity to come out to his place and practice!

Of course, I had no shearing equipment. I learned that Fred Schilling had a shearing outfit for sale, so I went out and bought that and planned on going the next day out to Robert Richards' and hone up on my shearing skills. Well, I had never sheared a sheep nor even saw one sheared! I got out to Bob's the next morning at nine o'clock.

Well, I worked my head off trying to get the wool off a nice yearling wether lamb (a neutered male), and by noon it was obvious that I should tie up the wether and go into the house for dinner so that both I and the sheep could rest up. It wasn't until about five in the afternoon that I finally got an acceptable amount of wool off that sheep! What to do! Bob suggested I contact Walter Steger, an expert shearer who did custom shearing. Yes, Walter would take the job, and he also offered to teach me the art of shearing! I had monkeyed around the better part of a day with one of Bob's sheep, and when Walter Steger came out to my place the next day he sheared a sheep in less than five minutes!

I'm glad I learned to shear sheep—I developed a really great appreciation for this highly skilled art! You don't just pick away with the clipper like you might do on a cow or a horse. Every stroke of the clipper is planned and memorized, it truly is an art! It was a satisfaction to learn, though I never was able to shear more than 65 sheep in a day. Walter could shear 100 a day, and if the weather was right—I mean, hot—that was like putting oil on the clipper, and then Walter could do 150 sheep in one day.

Well, I was learning and increased my flock to 250 ewes. I did well on the sheep, to the point where my father wanted to get some, too. We kept sheep for over 20 years and did well on them. We sold the lambs on the market for meat and sold the wool to a wool buyer for clothing.

My father was watching the newspaper for any sales that featured sheep, and found an auction listing a number of sheep scheduled to lamb at the same time as mine, and that sounded like a good thing to look into. The sale was up at Hewitt, Minnesota.

Well, my father went up to the sale, liked the looks of the sheep and bought around 50 of them! They were really a good-looking flock. The ewes were large Suffolk/Hampshire cross. They were good mothers and usually had twins and were good milking, so their lambs did well. Dad was quite pleased with his purchases. We were all happy!

It is interesting to note that sheep had been a factor in naming our farm Lawndale. It happened like this: in the early days when my Grandfather Ekberg first settled here, he made the acquaintance of James J. Hill, "The Empire Builder", as Herman was at the end of the railroad for a time. Mr. Hill was instrumental in bringing good purebred livestock to the area. He specifically promoted good Percheron horses, shorthorn cattle, Duroc-Jersey hogs, and Shropshire sheep.

Because of Mr. Hill's influence, many people availed themselves of the opportunity to get the excellent livestock promoted by Mr. Hill, and my grandfather was among them. He got the Percheron horses, the shorthorn cattle, and the Duroc-Jersey hogs. But he did not take any sheep because he did not like sheep!

Mr. Hill noted that Grandfather had not taken any sheep, and asked how come. It was not unusual that Mr. Hill asked, because he had come to know my grandfather quite well. Grandfather was not only very active in the community, he was also a Grant County commissioner. Mr. Hill had hosted my grandfather at his home in St. Paul, Minnesota, and was well aware that my grandfather was very much impressed with the very beautiful lawn at Mr. Hill's home. They had discussed what type of grass he had, etc., and how that could possibly be duplicated at the Ekberg's property in his new home in rural Herman.

Mr. Hill talked Grandfather into getting a flock of sheep to keep the grass mowed with very little effort and at the same time raise a fine crop of lambs. Grandfather went for Mr. Hill's idea and did get a very fine lawn, which was kept neatly trimmed by the sheep. Grandfather was really quite proud of his new home with its beautiful lawn, and urged Mr. Hill to come up and see it!

Well, Mr. Hill had a lot to do and had a lot on his mind, so he could not come until his business permitted him to do so. Grandfather was persistent and asked repeatedly and at length. Things were going on at Lawndale—the beautiful spring weather prompted my grandfather to have his sons—there were three of them in their teens and preteen years—take the storm windows off and put on the summer window screens.

That seemed like a good idea, and so in the usual sequence of that procedure they removed the storm windows and put them in the storage bin that housed the screens in the fall and winter months. It was a common practice that the screens, which had collected dust and dirt over the winter, were placed on the lawn where they were swept and dusted off. The boys had just put the last of the screens on the lawn when Grandmother, who had done some fresh baking, decided to reward the boys for working hard by having them in for morning lunch. The efforts of removing the storm windows had well prepared the boys for that kind of reward, and so they were only too glad to accept and went into the house.

The sheep, which were in the meadow at the time the boys went into the house, chose to come home just after the boys went in. The sheep noticing the screens came up to investigate; seeing that no one was around, they stepped on all the screens—not one was spared from this catastrophe. The boys were shocked when they came out, and Grandfather was furious!

Grandfather, who had never really been too keen about keeping the sheep on the lawn trimming detail, ordered the boys to haul the sheep into town to the stockyards, where they were shipped to the Cities! Without the sheep, the lawn grew long and rank. Grandfather was glad the sheep were gone—until a letter came to him from Mr. Hill informing him that his schedule was easing up and he wanted to see the beautiful lawn and new home. He would be up to observe the next week!

Grandfather immediately took the night train to the Cities to get a lawnmower! He was back the next day with a lawnmower, and the three boys were ordered to clean up the unmowed lawn. What a mess! One boy steered with the handle, and the other two were in front like a team of horses! You see, with all the tall grass it was a regular nightmare to mow. The boys had to back up and go ahead again and again. They had to mow it twice right away to make it look decent, so by the time Mr. Hill came, it looked pretty good again. The three Ekberg boys—Walter, Irven and Ray—thought the farm should have a name in honor of Mr. Hill's visit, so it was named *Lawndale Farm*!

Well, that pretty much explains why my Father did not like sheep. However, my having very good success for a number of years when I went into the sheep business was a compromise. We all finally came to liking and enjoying sheep.

History books note that sheep were the animals with the Golden Hoof, and were considered the Advance Guard of Civilization. The chair of England's Prime Minister was covered with a woolen sheep skin to remind him that the economy of the British Empire was founded on the sheep business. I've even heard that mutton is the only meat that can be served at an international event, as everybody can eat it!

I used to help the 4-H young people "block" their sheep for the fair. It was something that I liked to do and did for years. "Blocking" a sheep is the process of giving a sheep or lamb a beauty treatment before a sheep show or sale so that they show their best points. The result is a two-inch fleece of wool, which a skilled "blocker" can shape like frosting on a cake. It is not done as much nowadays, because judges prefer to have the animal completely shorn a couple of weeks before showing so the body conformation is more evident.

Showing sheep was something I enjoyed. The breeds I finally ended up with were *Columbia*, a white-faced breed noted for excellent wool production and a good meat carcass. The other breed I had was a black-faced meat-type of sheep—good-looking sheep that had no wool on their legs and head, so they really looked pretty sharp with their white woolly body and skinny black legs and head.

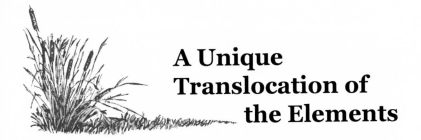

A Unique Translocation of the Elements

In my lifetime, I have witnessed some most unusual solutions to the simplest things!

This rather strange but certainly most simple and undramatic happening occurred a number of years ago on our farm when we were raising hogs. Hogs were one of those enterprises that if you choose to be in the business of the hog raising, then you get into it with the intention of raising a regular number of hogs for market and try to maintain a standard number year after year. Do not try to guess the anticipated market price, or alter the number of breeding animals to hold over from year to year.

If we thought the market would go down, and thus cut back the number of breeding animals held over that year, we could guess wrong. If we cut the size of the breeding herd, prices would generally go down and we would not have a good number of market hogs for sale. This was a common occurrence across the nation, because hogs were one of the enterprises that one could easily raise or lower the breeding herd. The reason was that hogs could average eight or nine piglets per litter and easily have two or three litters per year. In contrast, cows and sheep usually have only one or two offspring per birthing and usually give only one birth per year. Sheep could have two births per year. Cattle could not because of the longer gestation period.

When we had hogs, we went for two litters per year. We generally raised 800 to 1,000 hogs for the market per year. We grew our own hog feed and processed it on the farm, that is to say we ground our own grain and added vitamins, minerals and the recommended protein supplement—such as soybean meal—to complete the ration. We purchased the vitamins and minerals from feed companies. That is the subject of this chapter.

With our large number of hogs, it was necessary to grind and process hog feed on a weekly basis the year around. That required us to maintain the supply of vitamins and minerals. We kept a sufficient amount on hand so that we would never run out ... hopefully.

Harold Kietzman, a friend and neighbor, was the feed salesman who had encouraged us to try some of his brand of concentrates and minerals. He stopped by one day before the Easter holidays to see how the supplement was working out for us. I invited him into the barn to take a look, and to my horror the "look" showed that something was wrong. The lot of 80 market hogs looked scruffy and rough. I had not checked the barn lately, being occupied elsewhere and leaving the care of the pigs up to Jim, the neighbor kid who worked for us and had proven to be reliable in the past. For that reason, I had not looked in at the hogs daily as my habit was.

That evening when Jim came for evening chores, I asked him how everything was going, to which he answered, "Fine."

I told him that the hogs were not doing well, and asked if there was a change in the new feed that was being ground. And he said, "No, everything was the same."

However, then he got to thinking it over and said, "Gordon, I was going to mention it, I did have a mishap when I ground feed three days ago ... the additives come in different containers and when I was going to add the minerals it slipped out of my hands and scattered all over the ground in the mud. I couldn't pick it up and thought that the pigs are getting so much feed and missing out on the minerals this one time should not make any difference, but it appears that it did. So I decided I better tell you about it. I'm sorry!"

Well, I told Harold Kietzman about it and he said that he would call the company right away and have an extra container of minerals sent up from the factory down in southern Nebraska. Well, the solution sounded simple enough, but it was Easter weekend and it seemed everyone was on vacation. All storehouses around the country were out of any extra bags of minerals. After two full days of phone calling, no mineral was available. What to do.

Harold called me and said that the head feed man for the Triple "F" Feeds would talk to me about a possible solution. It wasn't long and a most kind and friendly man called me on the phone and apologized all over the place. He asked if we lived in the part of the country that had been subjected to severe dust storms of the 1930s and did it deposit banks or drifts of dust.

I said, "Yes, indeed, that was exactly what had happened as many pasture fences had almost been obliterated. Livestock such as cattle, horses, hogs and sheep were walking right over the fence."

He replied, "Just what we want!" He continued, "Now get a couple of five-gallon pails and a shovel. Fill the pails with dirt from the fence line, then slowly and carefully add it to your feed. You are going to hope that there is sufficient mineral that accumulated in those old sand banks that will make up for the minerals in the mineral bag that your helper had a mishap with."

I said, "For goodness sake, why in the world would I buy mineral from you people when I have drifts out here for free?"

The old feed scientist laughed and said, "You had better hope that is true."

It was, and in a few days with the dirt from the fence line in the feed the hogs were back to normal! The old scientist asked, "Where do you think we get mineral from? Yes, from the earth!"

Well, what a surprise, but I guess that I should have known that! The old scientist elaborated after asking, "When a unit train is shipped out of your town, what goes with the kernels of grain is vitamins, minerals, etc. That is why good farmers add fertilizer to their crops when they seed them in the spring."

A good lesson about the translocation of the elements!

Eggs

The only thing that I haven't written about is the domestic poultry. We did have a lot of domestic poultry at one time—up to 1,800 laying hens. That was a job—feeding the hens and gathering the eggs, then washing and packing the eggs into cartons.

Back in the early 1930s when we had a lot of chickens, egg prices had taken a tumble. I remember it well because my dad had cleaned and packed two double cardboard cases of eggs to sell or trade for groceries. That was a significant piece of work, as each double case held 360 eggs. You can imagine the long and sullen face on my dad when he had to bring the eggs home again, unsold.

I remember the occasion quite well because my little cousin, Jean Rae, was visiting here that day and we had to destroy all the eggs that had been sent home. Not a shell could be unbroken, not a membrane unbroken. Why? Because the eggs would start to rot and create sanitation problems, and we could not tolerate the smell. My dad had thought that my cousin and I would delight in smashing eggs, something different that might appeal to us three- and four-year-old children. It was fun at first, but we soon tired of the project and devised something else to get rid of the eggs. We put them down an old sewage stand pipe.

Geese

I have told how I got all my waterfowl—except my geese. That is rather strange, because I think it was geese that first attracted my attention. I first saw geese when going over to my Grandpa Gord's to visit. It was an easy thing to do, because the best short cut was through our neighbor's yard. Annie (Mrs. August) Fleischfresser was one of the most successful poultry raisers around. Part of the fun of going over to Grandpa Gord's place was going through the Fleischfresser's yard and seeing what new feathered creature Annie had hatched now. I really took a liking to their geese, but it was a different neighbor lady who made my wish for a flock of geese come true!

Lily Gilbertson gave me five goose eggs to set under a chicken hen. Was I ever thrilled! I was so happy I could hardly contain myself. I think I hatched four goslings out of the five eggs, and my goose flock grew from that humble beginning.

Most people usually kept a breeding flock of five geese, usually there were four hens and a gander (a male bird.) A large bird like a goose usually laid an egg every other day, but some rather faithfully laid one every day. I really didn't get into any big goose production until Senator Wayne Olhoft and I went into partnership and raised 1,300 geese and 200 Pekin ducks. The real miracle occurred when Senator Olhoft and I decided to process them all at the farm. Here is how that happened.

Senator Olhoft and I had volunteered to host the Midwest Goose Producers' Picnic at the farm. That was the project, but it turned into a really first class production, with the help of neighbors and friends, plus the use of their ovens, with several geese being roasted around the neighborhood. How in the wide world did the Senator and I decide to process over 1,500 geese and ducks? The neighbors must have thought we were crazy or on the brink of going crazy. Well, it was really not something that we planned to do. It just happened.

In the early 1970s, Senator Olhoft and I put on that real doozy of a picnic featuring roast goose and all the trimmings when we hosted a group of some 70 or 80 members of the Midwest Goose Producers. But we also had some unexpected guests—the commercial goose processors. It so happened that I was talking unseen behind a bush with a fellow producer, when I overheard a couple of the processors discussing the goose crop. One said he thought that it was excellent and with that many geese in the country, they could dare to drop the price in purchasing the live birds from the producers by a least a dime a pound!

I was so delighted to hear the scheming going on at the picnic that I told the Senator that maybe we should hold off on signing a contract with them until later on, so we decided not to sign or sell. They had figured that we were stuck and would be forced to sign with them as the middle man. Instead, we enlisted the help of friends and neighbors; we processed the birds ourselves and got a better price doing the job right on the farm. So, that is how we ended up processing our own birds. Producing, processing, selling direct to customers, and wholesaling to grocery stores and restaurants in the Twin Cities paid off. A crew came daily and feasted on goose cooking in the oven plus the trimmings, enjoying some of the fruit of their labor as they went. The meal was always delicious and a hit with the workers. It made for a nice local industry.

Incidentally, during the early years of our partnership I became Wayne's campaign manager for his run in the Democratic Party for the Minnesota Senate. He won against a seasoned incumbent and became Minnesota's youngest Senator.

Trapping 101
Mice and Weasels, Muskrats and Mink and Fox

I believe I always was infatuated with trapping. I loved the wild fur-bearers. Not only were they beautiful in their own right, they were smart and intelligent in relation to their habitat and environment. To catch them in a trap was indeed a challenge. Some species were more difficult to trap than others. Then there was the beauty of the habitat and outdoor environment. While I did receive various amounts of money at times, that was not my reason for trapping. I was so impressed by the creatures of the wild and their environment and I forever needed to have my attention drawn back.

So what was my first target? Would you believe it was a mouse? We had mice that started to get into our house in the fall of the year when the first cooler wave of air prompted them to get ready for winter. As a young four-year-old kid, my mother got me the paraphernalia—such as traps, bait and a few lessons on how to go about setting out my trap lines. Doesn't sound too exciting, but for a four-year-old kid it was not boring and the mouse habitat did include a cookie jar that both the trapper (me) and the target (the mouse) were wanting to get into! Anyway I did learn to remove the mice from the house and had fun doing it, which included my mother opening the cookie jar for me, not for the mouse, and giving me a nickel for each mouse caught!

Time went on and I became proficient in catching weasels, which were frequently in our chicken house. It was interesting to me that as I got older, there was someone to teach me the art of catching each animal that I progressed to. At about 12 years of age, the next species I was going to trap was muskrats! Growing up in the late 1930s, all I ever knew about muskrats was from the stories Dad had told me. I had not ever seen one, and here I was about 11 or 12 years of age. From the time I was ten, it was my idea that muskrats had left the area for good.

And then one day after school, my dad came home from town with the news that "King" Westin, a local hunter, had asked to trap muskrats in our slough of about 100 acres. I was shocked, because I had not heard of there being any muskrats around. Most of the ponds or sloughs had dried up through the dry years of the 1930s and there was no habitat for them anywhere around.

But now in the late 1930s, water was finally collecting in the low places again. The cattails and the bulrushes, whose root systems supplied food for the muskrats, were growing again and the muskrats were coming back! "King" Westin told my dad that he would trap on shares with us, and would give us one third or one fourth of the rats he caught. The DNR had many restrictions in place so the breed stock for the next year would not be depleted.

First, chopping open the muskrat houses was not allowed. When the ponds and sloughs froze over with ice, how else could we get to the muskrats? Well, we had to have a good ice chisel and we had to trap in wooden boxes on the ice. We noted when the ponds froze over enough so a person could safely walk on the ice. Then we could go and check just where the muskrats entered their houses under the ice. If rats were going in, the entrance could be located by noting a number of streams of bubbles under the ice. Then we would chisel about a five-inch hole in the ice right on top of the "bubble channel."

Next, we placed a wooden box with one half submerged into the water and one half above the water. The first half was where the unsuspecting muskrat would enter under water and then climb up to the top half, which was a ledge covered with a pad of dried moss. On top of the moss would be a #1 or #1½ jump trap. Some people also enticed the rats to crawl into the traps by putting in slices of carrots, apples or celery. This worked pretty well, and we were very sure that we had the hole at least 10 feet from the muskrat house. This worked well, but in spite of the trapping the muskrats increased rapidly! So the DNR started relaxing the rules already by the second year.

Muskrats were mainly active during the hours of darkness. However, our muskrat trapline had to be tended twice each day, as we caught many muskrats as they were feeding on nice sunshiny days. I had trapped 200 to 400 muskrats, and was able to sell them for $1.40 to $2.50 a piece after the pelt was skinned, stretched and dried.

The next species I learned to trap was the mink, and I did not do too well until someone had shown me some of the secrets of mink trapping. I know that a lot of expertise goes into setting a trap for mink. I never caught a lot of mink until I trapped with Clifford Jobst of Parnell, Missouri.

The summer I was 16, a transient farm worker came to Herman by hopping a ride on the freight train. There were about 50 or 60 transients in the park, all of whom had gotten there by hopping a freight train. My dad went in to see if he could find a couple extra farm workers for a couple of weeks, and Clifford was one of the couple of guys who caught Dad's eye. He hired him. Clifford worked for us through harvest and threshing and we got to know and appreciate him.

When we discovered that he had been a longtime trapper, it didn't take long for Clifford to offer to teach me some of the fine points of mink trapping in exchange for a few weeks of board and room. So our mink-trapping plans were made. Clifford would go to back to Missouri, and then a couple of weeks before mink season opened in November he woud drive back with his nephew, who was coming at that time to visit some relatives out in South Dakota. Clifford also planned to bring his dog, as the mink season at that time was open to taking mink by dogs.

So, I learned a considerable amount from Clifford about trapping mink, which I never forgot. From him I found out that if a mink got out of a trap, it would dive into the first hole it could see when it got free and would stay in that hole for as long as it took to heal an injured foot or leg. We were able to salvage a couple of mink that had escaped by using that information.

We did get a number of mink that fall, of which I received half. The weather was nice and we had some great success trapping, an outstanding time. Mink, however, was the only animal Clifford really knew anything about, but it was a great experience and happened right here at home.

Trapping season was something I always looked forward to each year. As the days got shorter and the weather got cooler—no, colder—I started thinking about trapping. The main reason for trapping when colder was because the weather caused the fur on fur-bearing animals to thicken, brighten up and get more luster. The cold weather caused the minks' fur to become just beautiful.

One interesting thing was how the fur buyers could tell if the trapper had "rushed" the season by setting traps too soon. The fur buyer would look at the inside of the proposed pelt to see if the mink hide was white down to the tips of the toes. As the weather cooled off in the fall, the fur (which is dark grey all summer long) starts to turn white. Thus it is generally white when the season opens, so a mark of a prime pelt is that the hide has turned from a dark grey to white, and the interesting thing is that the last part of the pelt to turn from grey to white is the feet—making it a "dead give-away" if it was trapped too early. If it was trapped too soon the feet on the pelt would be dark grey in color. Even waiting a couple of days before setting traps out could make a difference. No fur buyer wants to buy unprimed pelts.

My next venture in trapping was to learn about fox trapping, as the few fox I got were by accident and just chance happenings. I didn't know who to go to in order to find out about fox trapping. There was the added incentive that the fox pelts were bringing $85.

I thought and thought, asked a few questions—and then it occurred to me the answer was right under my nose. I was active in local government and I thought, *Isn't our county paying bounty on crows, pocket gophers and foxes... should I ask the county auditor who is getting the most fox in the county by trapping them? Just a simple question!*

I knew some made a practice of hunting by airplane, but I wanted to know who was the best fox trapper in Grant County. I went up to the County Auditor, whom I knew. I was not sure whether that was restricted information or not. You see with the prices being so high, I figured that it maybe was restricted information and no one would tell anything about fox trapping.

I asked the question, and the auditor was more than happy to tell me the name of the person who was doing the best job, so I contacted that person. I had made up mind that with fox prices being so good, I would be happy to pay and pay well for the privilege of finding out just how to trap fox. I thought to myself, *If he would teach me the art of fox trapping, I would be more than willing to give a few hundred dollars for the lessons!*

Well, yes indeed, he would teach me how to trap fox and was honored to be asked. No, he would not accept a large amount of money. All he was interested in was $25.00, to which I protested that was too little for teaching me that skill. That was the deal. He did not have a big area to trap in, and he seemed to insinuate that he encouraged the fox to come to him as that was how it certainly appeared. When I looked in his garage where he stored his furs after skinning and drying them, there must have been over 30 pelts in various stages of finish and it was only a few weeks into the season. I asked how many sites he had set and I thought that he had indicated about a half dozen, which I thought was remarkable!

He indicated about a two-mile radius from his trap sites, and that his sites drew the fox in from about two miles. Then he told me that if there was such a thing as a high hill close to a lake around my place, I should outfit myself with the following: a hatchet, a stubby shovel with an 18-inch handle, a box with a ¼-inch screen on the bottom, a pail of dry dirt, a scissors and a square of black plastic or a handful of sheep's wool. For each trap site I also should have a 16-inch welded trowel in a T-shape for a stake to anchor the trap, a jar of well-rotted ground stray cat, a dozen ear swabs and a small bottle of *All Call* fox lure. Plus, I should wear hip boots so I do not permeate the ground with human scent and have trapper's waterproof gloves.

Following his instructions, I found the hill or raised area, and from a distance decided how I would approach the proposed trap, making sure I came from due north from at least 50 feet from the trap site. Looking straight south, I selected a spot to conceal the set trap. Then I knelt down so I was comfortable while making the set and dug only a very shallow depression.

When the trap was set in the hole, I cut a piece of plastic or wool to place carefully within the jaws of the trap. It is necessary that the plastic or wool is within the jaws of the trap so the trap jaws do not throw dirt when the fox steps on the trap pan. Then I took a couple of small shovelfuls of dry dirt that I brought with me and put the dirt into the screened box, then ever so carefully I shook the box so the screened fine, dry dirt covered the trap.

Next, I made a small hole with the ear swab, off to the side of the trap and going in at an angle to add a small wad of the cat mixture along with a couple drops of the *All Call* scent. Each day when I checked my trap, I stayed back a few feet so I didn't spread scent. If I did this right, I would have a fox in a few days. If I was going to kill the fox, I made sure I shot it between the eyes with a .22 short, and was not afraid of getting blood on the ground—the more the better!

I have generally caught several fox at the same trap site. Do not use more than one of the #1½ double coil spring per site—one trap is enough if done right.

For mink and raccoon, use water sets or very carefully done dry sets. With a good dry set, use a stick or heavy cattail for a jumper! A jumper is something the animal might usually jump over, such as a cattail or cornstalk, and onto the trap.

The Bird Attack

A friend, who was my trapping partner at the time, and I would each check the traps close to home respectively and then travel together for the rest of the day, enjoying each other's company. One time, it was my turn to drive for the rest of the day. The first trap site we were going to check had the misfortune of having a female mink that had been caught a day before and was partially eaten by what we suspected could have been a great horned owl. I had done a good job of resetting the trap, and hoped that whatever had taken the mink would get in the trap that day.

The trap site was on an abandoned road through a marsh. I said I would drive around the marsh and walk out on the ice to the trap site, which was about in the middle of the marsh. My friend elected to stay in the car and wait for me, as it seemed I was not likely to have anything in the trap after just removing the mink that the owl had gotten yesterday. But, lo and behold, when I got nearly to the trap site I could see something caught in it. Yeah. We had apparently caught the owl that had gotten the female mink the day before, and was that owl ever angry! It was caught by one leg and trying to get away, and getting angrier all the time.

I decided to see if I could knock the owl unconscious and release it. The thought was appropriate and a good idea, but it didn't work out that way. I did knock the owl out with my trapper's hatchet, but when I knelt down on one knee to release it, the owl "came to" and attacked me with its claws on the leg that was not in the trap. It grabbed me just above the knee, sending its claws through clothing and hip boots. I could feel the claws going into my flesh and was it ever painful! (The claws must have penetrated one of my blood veins, because there was well over a cupful of blood in my boot, which kept sloshing about all the way back to the car.)

After the owl attacked me, I was not going to attempt to kindly release it again and get another battle scar. I grabbed my trapline .22 revolver out of my holster and dispatched the owl.

Church

As I mentioned earlier, my ancestors were Scandinavian, having immigrated from Sweden on my father's side of the family and from Norway on my mother's side of the family. We were a happy family and got along well together. There was no evidence of that old humorous cliché that went "ten thousand Swedes ran through the weeds a 'chased by one Norwegian." Well, that was really not true of our family. Thank goodness, we all got along well together.

At that time, the churches were very cliquey—for example, there were Swedish Lutheran churches, Norwegian Lutheran, German Lutheran, Finnish Lutheran, etc. I was introduced to a class of four year olds in the kindergarten room of Augustana Swedish Lutheran Church.

The main thing I remember about that Sunday School of over 80 years ago was that my mother dressed me in short pants called knickers, which they thought were "cute." Well, I didn't think they were "cute" then and I still don't.

Mrs. Orton Gillen taught the class for a number of years and was a wonderful teacher. I made my way through the classes and it was discovered that I had a gift for memorization. As a result, I was assigned a significant part in the children's Christmas program (Luther's second article of the Creed and explanation, and I still remember it!). It was awhile before I truly realized that memorization was a gift; I thought everyone could memorize easily. I memorized because I enjoyed it, it was fun!

I was often called upon to do memory work in poems and plays and got great enjoyment out of doing that, especially when I received compliments. I was really glad to oblige! Doing a thing that one likes to do, whether it be eating, drinking, speaking or what have you, was really honoring a person by highlighting one's "gift" and so it was that it was quite natural that I found public speaking more and more enjoyable.

Of course, I gradually realized that public speaking was my gift and asked God to help me improve upon my ability and thanked God. And so it was that my field of public speaking grew to include pulpit supply for churches as well as speaking at funerals and eulogies, etc., where a message needed to be delivered. I think I easily could say that I spoke at or helped out at well over 400 funerals and the like in over 60 years. I enjoyed every minute of it! I served the Odd Fellow Lodge by attending 176 meetings throughout the state as Grand Master from 1962-1963. I served on a number of local boards as well.

My Dream

I was a high school drop-out. I don't know that anything bothered me more. I'll never forget the day I dropped out of Herman High School. I had thought about it a lot, and we had many different neighbors call on us begging me NOT to drop out of high school. There were letters from my two aunts, one being my dad's sister, Effie, who was a high school teacher on the Iron Range at Mountain Iron, Minnesota. She told me I would regret that decision all my life, and that my health was the only legitimate reason for doing so. Well, I was not feeling well at times, but I thought that I could really handle it.

Then my other aunt, my mother's sister, Helen, who worked in the city, took a couple days off work and came home to urge me to continue my schooling. Well, things were hard when she was growing up and it was difficult to find money to go to school. She told me how she had cried when her father, my grandfather, had lost his wife from tuberculosis. Grandpa could not afford to run the farm without her, so Aunt Helen had to stay home and help.

I still thought of withdrawing from school, but I felt guilty about it. Two of my teachers, Mrs. Cosh, my English teacher, called on my folks and urged me to continue in school, and then Mrs. Van Zomeren, my biology teacher, visited with my folks at PTA.

It wasn't difficult for me to learn. You see, I had A's and B's on my report card. Well, we just let things slide for a while.

One day I was doing veterinary work on one of the cattle I had lassoed. I was not near a post or fence, so I tried hanging on as I worked my way over toward something that I could tie to the end of the rope while I doctored the animal. However, it took a lot longer to subdue the animal—I was exhausted, and had a pain in my chest. Well, I had almost fainted from the pain in my chest, so my folks took me to Dr. Gruenwald in Hoffman. He thought that, all things considered, it appeared there was too much stress for me in school. He suggested I take a couple of days off from school so I could more correctly decide if I felt better without the schooling. So I just never went back to school, and I felt that I had let my parents down. I never forgot that.

I didn't go to many events, so my parents urged me to join the Odd Fellow Lodge because there were a number of neighbors that belonged. Well, I started going to lodge as there were several young guys my age, and I started to enjoy it. A few years went by and I went to an Odd Fellow state convention and met people from all over the state. I thought that was not only fun, but interesting.

Then as I learned more about lodge, I found out about the Encampment, which was a military branch of the IOOF. Mr. Orin Slocum of Madelia wanted to nominate me for the Encampment Office and I said, "Yes," but I didn't get elected. The next year they wanted to nominate me again and I decided to try once more. I won. I was started on a line office, which meant I would have to try for three offices and serve for a year in each before I finally could be the head of it after four years. In the end I was elected The Grand Patriarch of the Grand Encampment of the Odd Fellows of Minnesota.

Well, I did a good job and served the Encampment faithfully. It happened that one of the International Officers had deliberately committed an error in his office, and since I had done such a good job as the Grand Patriarch of the Encampment I was asked to consider running for Grand Master of the Grand Lodge of the Odd Fellows of Minnesota. I really was not interested in devoting another whole year to the Odd Fellows because I had a farm to run.

Not only that, I had 240 ewes as a part of my farming operation. These sheep were scheduled to give birth to their lambs starting on January 15th. Knowing they were going to give birth in January, I needed to have heated quarters for them as the lambs are quite tender. They are generally scheduled to give birth in May when the weather is warm. Also, I had to consider that when I confined my flock in January because of the cold, the mother sheep had to be confined to a small pen for a couple of days so that the lamb could nurse its mother. Anyway, it should be thoroughly draft free for the lamb after birth and the lamb needs to get some milk in its stomach. Thus, there must be constant supervision of the flock. Without a good shepherd, one could almost certainly count on losing a number of lambs.

So, what to do. Friend and Odd Fellow brother Bob Richards could see that it was impossible for my older father to handle that many animals, so he called some of the younger lodge members to see if they could help. A two- or three-man crew came every day and helped my dad. Without that crew, it would have been impossible. As it turned out, only 12 of the 240 ewes had single lambs, with all others having twins or triplets. Final tally for that lambing season was just over a 200% lamb crop. Amazing!

And that was not the only thing that the lodge brothers did. Always ready to help whenever needed, I really have to give the lodge credit for what they did. I should really say that the Harmony Lodge of Herman, Minnesota, went through the chair of the Grand Master, not Gordon Ekberg.

So what did I do that year? I attended approximately 176 meetings, and signed up two candidates for membership, Peter Noreen and Russell Gilbertson. I believe I was only late for one or two meetings. Only three people attended the first informational meeting that I spoke at, but a few months later there were about 300 people out at a St. Louis Park meeting.

I had spent a full week preceding the Grand Lodge meeting building a promotional booth on the mezzanine floor of the convention hotel to showcase the projects the Odd Fellows promoted. The annual

Grand Lodge Convention was well attended, with a packed house. I should mention that I had several standing ovations during my speeches at the Convention, and spoke for about an hour without notes.

The highlight of the convention was the opening night, which was certainly well put together by my mentor and Master of Ceremonies, James S. Lombard, of Northrup Auditorium of the University of Minnesota. Included in the audience that night right down in the front row were seated some folks who were very special to me: my parents, Aunt Helen, and her household employer, Mrs. J.C. Litzenberg, at whose home I was always a welcome guest when staying in Minneapolis.

Also present were the Representative of the Sovereign Grand Lodge, and the Deputy Sovereign Grand Master, C. Everett Murphy from Kingfisher, Oklahoma, who had just arrived that morning after attending a meeting of the Sovereign Grand Lodge in Baltimore, Maryland. As C. Everett Murphy was about to speak, he knowingly caught the eye of Dr. Lombard, then proceeded to announce that at the meeting in Maryland the executive board had commented on Brother Gordon Ekberg's efforts in Minnesota, and had said that Brother Ekberg was the "outstanding Grand Master on the North American Continent." My folks' as well as Mrs. Litzenberg's and Auntie Helen's mouths flew open and "tears of joy flooded all of our faces." There was a standing ovation and thunderous applause.

I was thrilled as I thought back to the day that I became a high school drop-out. I felt that this moment made up for that disappointment. I was the object of many congratulations that evening and for days afterward. I really appreciated the year that I served as Grand Master.

"Between the Cattails and the Bulrushes"

A Poem by Gordon Ekberg

Between the Cattails and the Bulrushes
Where a froggy's life begins
Where the merganser chases the minnow
And the minnow chases the bug!

Where there is courtin' and a'sportin'
Of ducks of most every kind
Where there's logs, and bogs, and pollywogs
And many other things you'll find.

The frogs and toads are a'greetin' and a'eaten'
Insects of every kind, and the insects will surely take a'beatin',
Tis' without a doubt nor reason as it really is the season
For an insect banquet feastin'.
Their amphibian larder is without a doubt, a reason to work a little harder
To fill the mutual larder without a chance to barter.

The worth of a billion golden guineas
Are what the wetlands do for free
For the likes of you and me!
There are grasses and sedges along the water edges
Also, rushes and brushes
To hold it all in place without a trace of a brace,
For Uncle Sam's Peace!

With over 900 species of fish and fowl and amphibians
and beneficial insects too
Who need a wetland's habitat for their home.
Oh, a million golden guineas could hardly even rate
for a fraction of the action
Of the wetlands of this State!

And then those magnanimous sentinels of the
Wetlands strike their blows on pollution
With a solution on pollution.

There's frogs and toads and yes, there's roads
Thousands of Golden Guineas.
There's barrels of snails
And there's shrubs and grubs and all kinds of muds.
Like a rug over waters, the lemna dodders.

Save the wetlands and make some bucks
Drain the pothole and lose some bucks as well as ducks,
And maybe save ducks.

Soft as a sponge for flood water retention,
Preserve some habitat
For more muskrats to trap
So the water don't 'vaporate and the puddles do not go!

Dragon flies and insects live in wetlands
You know and annually emerge with
A flourish of style to make our life more worthwhile!

A canvasback builds a nest of cattails
And rushes to enhance the landscape,
And cherish our thought.

There's blooms and plumes and shotgun booms
There's death and destruction as well as birth and eruption
Also gads of construction.

With the dawn it's gone
It seems to light a spark, such as was found on the ark
They ravage the marsh like squishing a squash,
God made the wetlands as he did you and me
For a purpose and a "need" it is true indeed!
And on it the environment, it will feed,
A nest will do it best.
A promise, a deed will fulfill a need!

It's all in the reed, if you plant the seed
How deft is the reft?
If things are done well, it's as clear as a bell,
Whether we gyrate or gravitate, it's up to us.

It grows like a weed it you plant this seed
Are you ready for more or are you going to close the door?
It filters the pollution and that's the solution.
The creator has spoken, it's us that have
Broken promises and creeds to fulfill the wetland needs.

We put up too much dilution to have a good solution
For a million golden guinea as would
Hardly even rate for a fraction of the last
Of the action of the wetlands of this State!
For there is wild rice and mice and other things,
Rodents galore for food for hawks and owls and other fowls as well!
Wild turkeys too.

If you hunt the goose and even the moose to make your larder swell
And a nice big nest of turtle's eggs rest in a nest of sand
Spawning fish will grant your wish as well.

The promise is certainly to reclaim and maintain the wetlands
And enlarge them which we can
Both the quantity and quality will really fill the bill
Enhancing biological diversity is really in the mill,

For between the cattails and the bulrushes is what
We wish to do and we shall, we will!
For it's NOT a bitter pill.

"Between the Cattails and the Bulrushes"

—A Column for *APWS Magazine*
(Americican Pheasant and Waterfowl Society)

Almost 40 years ago, I decided to write a column on ducks and waterfowl. Little did I realize that I couldn't write about waterfowl without getting water involved, and of course the wetlands.

In fact, when I wrote about waterfowl I was soon writing about wetlands, much to the delight of my personal friend Muggs Townsend of Fergus Fall, Minnesota. He was a great outdoorsman and started a club that had as its motto, "Save the Wetlands."

It was, of course, diametrically opposed to another group whose motto was "Drain the Pot Holes." Their motto encouraged drainage of the wetlands, which was a loss not only for waterfowl but for crucial habitat for some 900 species of birds, fish, amphibians and beneficial insects necessary for recharging ground supplies and helping to ensure pure water for the humans who drank it!

The wetlands did a magnificent job of filtering surface water on its way back into the aquifer. If man should be successful in his misguided effort to decimate the wetlands, then what would it take to filter and purify river water that is now cleaned up by wetlands?

I have tried to write a little "jingle" that would really be impressed upon your mind and soul. Now remember that this is essentially what the Corps of Engineers and the agricultural interests are trying and have been trying for years to do—to eliminate the wetlands that serve as an incubator for all the 900 species that call the wetlands home. It also serves as a buffer strip to prevent flash floods from destroying your homes and inundating the agricultural lands for food-production.

The jingle:

A million Golden Guineas would hardly even rate
For the fraction of the cost of the action of the wetlands of this State
God made the wetlands as He did for you and me
For a purpose and a need, it's true indeed!
And on it the environment, it will feed.
If things are done well, it is as clear as a bell
That between the cattails and the bulrushes are the plants we need!
Also, there's shrubs and grubs and all kinds of mud
For it filters the pollution and that's the solution
The Creator has spoken, it's us that have broken
Promises and creeds for futile needs and have
Too much dilution to have a good solution
Between the cattails and the bulrushes, those
Magnanimous Sentinels of the wetlands strike
Their blows on pollution with a solution for politicians.
The frogs and toads are eatin' loads of insects of every kind!
On those logs and bogs and pollywogs you'll find.

Bulletin of the
Minnesota Pheasant & Waterfowl Society
A Bimonthly Publication

Published 13 Feb. 1982
Vol. 9, No. 1

Between the Cattails and the Bulrushes

by Gordon Ekberg

"What a pretty duck. Surely we are not going to eat it!" That was back in 1933, just before Thanksgiving and my father had just bought four Greenhead drakes from my uncle. The drakes were intended to be table-fare on special occasions. But the Ekberg's four year old son, Gordon, was thoroughly captivated by the beauty of the Rouen (the domestic counterpart of the Mallard) drakes. I begged and pleaded to have one for a pet... no, better yet..."Can't we keep two, a mommy and a daddy and then maybe we can have some little ducks on our pond next summer." My father relented gave me two of the Greenhead drakes plus a discourse on the fact that a mommy duck was called a hen and was brown in color. It was agreed that if I took good care of the drakes, one could be traded to my uncle for a hen along come spring. My father's thinking, I learned in later years, was that I would soon tire of the birds and they could be butchered at a later time. That was a little over forty-eight years ago, a lot of water has flowed between the cattails and the bulrushes, but I'm still captivated by waterfowl of all kinds.

I told Don and Joan that I would try to write a regular column for them. I told them that I really have no special qualifications for writing (a statement that time will reveal as being uneccessary, in fact you may even realize I have none by the time you finish the column), but that I would write until such time as someone else volunteered. In writing this, I feel somewhat like the fellow who perished in the terrible Johnstown, Penn. flood. When he arrived in Heaven he immediately asked the Lord if he could address the assembly of Heaven on the over-whelming awfulness of the Johnstown flood. The Lord indicated that He didn't really think it was necessary, but the fellow was so persistant that he was finally granted permission to speak. The Lord called all the Assembly of Heaven together, the fellow could hardly wait for the Lord to introduce him so he could tell of the horrors that had engulfed Johnstown, as the Lord was finishing the rather brief introduction the enthusiastic fellow had already bounded to the podium and was looking out at the vast multitude of faces. It was at this point, having finished the introduction that the Lord leaned over and whispered in his ear, "Remember that NOAH is in the crowd!" I'm well aware of the many "Noahs" that we have in the bird business in our Minnesota Pheasant & Waterfowl Society and so I feel very humble as I embark on this project.

Well, I did take care of the ducks that winter of '33 and '34, and in about the haphazard manner that you might expect of a four and a half year old boy. My father did trade the extra drake for a hen and I was in the duck business. Spring brought a frenzied activity of pen building. There was so much activity in the pen that the hen never did settle down to her matronly duties of egg laying until, after several weeks of arranging and rearranging the pen and trying first one nest box and then another, I got disgusted from not seeing any eggs and directed my attention elsewhere. With peace and quiet finally reigning over the pen, the ducks got down to business, made a nest, laid it full of eggs and hatched some ducklings. I played with the ducklings until my parents, fearful that I would kill the ducklings by so much handling, suggested that I open the gate and let the little family enjoy the summer on the pond. There was little water in the pond during the dry years but the ducks made use of what little there was and grew to maturity.

Year followed year and I tried most varieties of domestic ducks and also raised Wild Mallards from nests found in the hay fields. A neighbor lady, Lily Gilbertson, gave me a setting of goose eggs when I was about ten and then I was in the goose business. Duck and goose eggs were generally gathered and set under "settin" hens and I thus earned my spending money, selling the birds to the local creamery in the fall. Since that rather small beginning, I have had waterfowl on the place ever since. There have been lean years and then years when we raised up to 1500 geese and 1000 ducks and with that many birds on the pond there were some mighty big spaces between the cattails and bulrushes.

Editor's Note: Gordon Ekberg is a farmer near Herman, Minnesota. He has been in the MP&WS approximately 4 years. Gordon enjoys hunting, fishing, trapping and camping. He was a national speaker for the Odd Fellows. He is a lay minister for the Methodist Church and teaches Sunday School. Gordon started raising domestic ducks in 1933 at the age of 4! Gay, Gordon's wife, is a Speech Therapist but now spends most of her time with their 4 children...Kris Ann 7, Amy 6, Joel 4, and Evangeline 2. She also enjoys sewing when she has time.

APWS
MAGAZINE
AMERICAN PHEASANT AND WATERFOWL SOCIETY

VOLUME 05, 12   JUNE

Between the Cattails and the Bulrushes

by Gordon Ekberg

John was grinning as he came hurriedly into the house!!! Now what I wondered?? "Dad" said John, "The swan is hatching!!!!" The culmination of four if not five years of concentrated effort had arrived and I too was grinning like a small kid!!!! What a wonderful event and a good feeling to know that I could also revert to the boyish thrill of the "hatchin"!!! What a time we have had getting this to happen!!! Do you remember back when the old female died and we got a new mate for the old Cob???? And we were so happy to have the good fortune of locating an older Pen so soon after the death of the old female and then about a week, ten days after the acquisition of the new mate, John found her dead one morning, the obvious victim of a severe beating!!! Then followed weeks of trial offerings of a new mate, all of which were rejected by what appeared to be a very persnickety old cob!!! Weeks dragged into months and still no sign that we were even somewhere close to appeasing the fine tuned marriageable tastes of the fussy cob!!! Then one day, I just happened to notice in the winter quarters where we now were that the old Cob was seemingly "giving the eye" to a very beautiful Super Dewlap African Goose Hen, yeah! A Domestic Goose, surely not, but by watching carefully, I could detect subtle, ever so slight advances that the African Female and the huge Male Trumpeter were paired off!!!! Who would ever have dreamed that, no wonder the old Cob refused the many offerings....he already had a mate!!! I will not go into the story of the effort that it took to separate the two lovers except to say that distance, hearing distance that is most important, say a mile or more and two or three is better!!!

Well, back to the story of the hatching! I asked John how many, but he said that it appeared that she had just started! The next day it appeared that way too! And the following day one little cygnet following the Cob appeared on the pond! This one little offspring seemingly was the full hatch for the year and that was the first time that we have had such a limited production. Checking back at the nest revealed that there were four eggs that did not hatch which John put in our incubator just in case. We will examine those before throwing them to see whether they had been fertile and the young had died in the shell or if they had never been fertile! This is the first production from this young Pen but in over forty years this is still unusual! Then because we were hoping for more eggs to hatch, John had not pinioned the cygnet and that proved a task of greater dimension than usual!!! John made his first attempt to capture the young cygnet when the parents came to shore to eat and the young swan was close to two weeks old and he forgot to allow for the extra speed and versatility that the young swan had acquired in the two weeks!! Needless to say, the young swan made good its escape! Two days later, reinforced with a boat and a pair of waders and a much longer handled dip net, John emerged the victor!!! John confirmed what he already knew, "Pinion as soon as the last cygnet has hatched" there is practically no blood and so-so-so much easier to catch! Of course it was not possible to do that this time.

The Nightly News on NBC has carried some of the most sobering reports on certain Herbicides used on corn and beans! It appears that the herbicide sprayed on herbaceous material will kill most everything except those plants that have been genetically altered to withstand the spraying! In this case corn and beans (Soybeans) are the crops that are genetically altered, and any plant not so treated has not a chance of surviving! Sometimes people who are ill informed think that is a good thing because we will get rid of all the weeds, well it just doesn't work that way because in the all out wholesale destruction of the weeds a number of beneficial plants and insects are destroyed as well! Honeybees are some of the "Good" insects being destroyed and take note that there are many other insects and plants in the "Good" category as well!!!! On an even more alarming note is the potency of the spray developed in the last few years has been that it "lasts" not just for hours, days or months as has been the case in the past BUT NOW SOME IS CAPABLE OF RETAINING ITS HIGHER POTENCY FOR UP TO THREE YEARS and further permeates into some of our food products themselves!!!!! Is it any wonder that many of the countries of the world will not allow some of these on their shores! As you drive across America these days, note how clean and free of weeds the fields are!!! If you think that is good, think again, and reflect on what I just informed you! Before this month ends we hope that more news of a happier vein light up the air waves of the world!

That is what I find out here between the cattails and the bulrushes!!!!

Trumpeter Swans at Lawndale Farm

Odd Fellows Song, With Recitation

By Gordon Ekberg

Tres Lachowitzer, singer from Herman, Minnesota, was asked to put this to melody. She chose the tune from the Battle Hymn of the Republic, *sung slowly, to accommodate each word per musical note.*

Throughout this wide creation, O'er Ev'ry land and sea,
Odd Fellows are touching hearts of those like you and me,
From Greenland's icy mountains, to the hills of Tennessee,
Odd Fellow Charity.

Refrain:
The Odd Fellows said: Yes, we will! (repeat 3 times)
Their Fellowship is marching on.

With Joy, its steps attending, guards the feet of youth,
From paths of sin and sorrow, by Friendship, Love, and Truth,
It still is marching on, its history's the truth.
Odd Fellow Charity.

Refrain
A place for all the aging, and the orphan's home to fill,
In Meadville, Pennsylvania, no other group could fill the bill,
No government, no religion, would design for aged or ill.
Odd Fellow Charity.

Refrain

When we all meet together, for counsel or for aid,
May the love of purest virtue, each member's heart pervade,
Love is the grand remedy, for all the social evil made.
Odd Fellow Charity.

Refrain

For all the good toward God or man, Our Father of love,
Our labors blessed and to our efforts, grant success above,
And to your honor we will raise, unceasing prayer and love.
Odd Fellow Charity.

Refrain

Recitation with song (*sing "Yes, we will"*):

It came to the loving Odd Fellows who said, "*YES, WE WILL!*"
Over half the fire departments west of the Mississippi heard, "*YES, WE WILL!*"

Some over 75,600 young people were instructed and educated in world government through a youth program touring New York City and international government agencies, when Odd Fellows again said, "*YES, WE WILL!*"

Odd Fellows and Rebekahs asked to set up education foundations, "*YES, WE WILL!*"

Every state, province and country set own education foundation, "*YES, WE WILL!*"

Yes, every place where the Odd Fellows' flag is flown, "*YES, WE WILL!*"
Norway operates Children's Village in El Salvador, "*YES, WE WILL!*"
United States operates Children's Villages in Cambodia, "*YES, WE WILL!*"

Europe setting up Children's Villages as needed, "*YES, WE WILL!*"

Visual Research Foundation with Johns-Hopkins, "*YES, WE WILL!*"

Norway Odd Fellows operate two lifesaving ships, "*YES, WE WILL!*"
Recitation (*sing refrain*):

One of the charter members of Herman, Dr. A.D. Larson, M.D., made the discovery in 1896 that many people were being injured while handling gasoline in cans. He was also serving in the Minnesota Legislature and felt that a warning was needed. Thus, he offered a bill that all cans for gasoline be painted red. The bill passed and became law and has since become copied worldwide.

Sherriff Wyatt Earp was a member.

Four United States presidents were IOOF members. Many Governors were, too.

The Rebekah sisters joined early on, 13 years before any other organization invited women to join.

Refrain

Originating in England in the early 1700s, Odd Fellowship was brought to America in 1819 and enjoyed a rapid growth never before seen in any organization nor group. Most everyone, political or common, rich man, poor man, made up the IOOF.

They escorted maids and ladies as nice as they could be ... the Rebekahs!
It was in days of old and knights were bold, and somewhat tough and rough and needed kindness, too, so brotherly love and good manners took off the crust and rust, and made a fine and gentlemanly to-do.
Neat and clean, right as rain, pleasant and mannerly, too.
To meet a man was generally a pain, but these were different, these were Odd Fellows.

Refrain

Gordon Ekberg, IOOF Grand Master of Minnesota
1962-1963

Finale

Between the Cattails and the Bulrushes

Where lovely water lilies grow

Where Jesus saves the sinner

And makes of him a winner!

For His saving grace is bold

And His Love will never grow old.

Remembrances of Dad

Given by Joel Ekberg, Amy Ekberg, and Kris Ann Erickson at Gordon's Funeral January 28, 2017

Joel:

My dad was involved in many things, if it was something in the community he probably was involved. I think that he liked to bring people together to share in a community.

My dad seemed like he could relate to almost anyone, because of his time with the Odd Fellows, traveling the state as Grand Master and also when running for Congress in a special session in 1977. He would meet someone, and would almost instantly know someone in that town/city and see if they had some mutual acquaintances, very good at networking.

Church and faith were very important to my dad. I remember numerous times where he did lay speaking, prayer services and some funerals. On some occasions when he did lay speaking I can remember my dad riding in the passenger seat, while Mom drove. He had his Bible, concordance and some scratch paper to get his sermon prepared on the way to the church. I remember coming downstairs in the mornings and see my dad reading the Bible. Honesty was one of the most important things that he taught me. My mom always said the man people knew was the man he was.

The outdoors/wildlife/hunting seems like they all tie together as one. I think it was the beauty of nature and the camaraderie of everyone that made these things all enjoyable. If a hunt wasn't successful in harvesting our game, it was still great to get out in God's earth and enjoy the simple things. Deer hunting was the best for me, hunting in the northwoods of Minnesota. Dad teaching me how to use a compass, make a one-match fire, carve a spoon out of a sapling to eat our baked beans that we would cook over the fire. Getting a lesson on how to gut my first deer.

Sports: My dad wasn't much into sports, but any sports that his kids were in he would come and watch some of our games. I remember once him going to a *Pheasants Forever* banquet and sitting next to some guy one night who was very interesting and they got along great with them both having great passion for wildlife. He came home and asked the hired man if he recognized the name the man had given him, because the man said it in a way that my dad thought that he should know who he was. His name was Bud Grant, head coach of the Minnesota Vikings.

Giving a 110%: Seemed like whatever my dad did, it was always more than average. I remember him being in charge of our Sunday school Christmas program. Everything was done, full costumes for everyone, numerous rehearsals, everyone memorizing their lines, extra props being built and painted, and even had me in a harness to come swinging down as an angel out of the heavens. A star that moved up to the front of the church. He did it because he wanted to give it his best.

Planning for the 1995 release of the Federal duck stamp was a local from the Cities, Jim Hautman. Jim had called and asked if Dad could set up a display for him for the release of the Stamp at the Mall of America. My dad said yes way more than no, and was happy to help a friend out. So Dad, John and I set about to prepare a display. Digging out cattails and bulrushes to put into plastic planters, a big metal pan that would serve as a small pond, green outdoor carpet to lay across the pond and to put water in, special green wire, along with a pair of live mallards as that what was on the Stamp, and freshly-hatched ducklings, too. When we were about done setting up in the Mall of America, a guy walks in and says, "Hey, Gordy how are you doing?" It was Senator Paul Wellstone.

Odd Fellows: He enjoyed it because of the enjoyment of meeting other people, the activities, the degree work, because it was for the community. He was really proud to have me join, and be able to attend meetings with him while I was in high school. He held many positions and had many awards. He would always have just a few words to say on a subject that would undoubtedly go for 10 minutes. He loved to talk, and had all kinds of ideas of how to get things accomplished. When I think of Odd Fellows, I think of Carmel Apples, Smelt, Fruit Cake, Hall of Fame, Ice fishing Derby. He did it all.

Dad always had the "can do attitude"—nothing too big that wasn't worth a try, sometimes questioning, "Why can't we do it?"

Memory: He could remember lineage on both sides of his parents, remember all these people everywhere, memorize the whole degree book for the Odd Fellows, which was always quite amazing, giving his one part, always a long piece, and rarely needed help. He could remember practically everything, which he claimed sometimes was not always good, some things he wished he could forget. Almost a photographic memory.

Farming: I remember many stories of people he had helped with their livestock doing veterinary work, just to help people out. He retired from farming in 1986 and focused full-time on the waterfowl and art gallery, which were his great interests, but when I had an interest in farming he took me to an auction in 7th grade and we bought a small disc for $200. He enjoyed driving and looking at my crops and always thought I did a good job of farming.

There are so many things that he did, and so many stories, that I could keep you all here for a couple hours, which would be alright with Dad I'm sure. It was a good, long, interesting life with many blessings.

Some of his sayings: if we would be working on something but not quite satisfied with the outcome, he would say "If you can do better, then do better." I remember not exactly knowing what it was I wanted to do in life, Dad would say, "Do something, God can only steer a moving ship." If I thought that something couldn't be done he would say, "You don't know, if you don't try." Another, "Don't slouch, shoulders back," and when we were in Deer Camp, when first light was breaking, "Daylight in the Swamp!" Now he's home, and he meant a lot of things to a lot of different people, but to me he will always be "Dad."

Amy:

Gordon F. Ekberg. Crop Farmer. Cattle Farmer. Duck Farmer. Community Leader. Odd Fellow. Lay preacher. Sunday School teacher. Bible study leader. Mentor. Teacher. Farm advocate. Political supporter. Hunter. Environmentalist. Writer. Small business owner of an art gallery, frame shop, waffle shop, and bed and breakfast. All these titles and he lived in one place, on one farm for his entire life.

My dad is a true example of the saying "Grow where you are planted." He lived his whole life on the farm built by his grandfather (Frank Ekberg) just five miles east of Herman. When railroad executive James J. Hill visited the Ekberg farm, he declared, "This is the most beautiful lawn in the hill and dale." The words "Lawn" and "dale" were extracted and put together and then on was known as "Lawndale Farm".

The farm was a place that has brought together family and friends alike through the years.

In his younger years, my father lived with his father and mother. His Grandfather Frank Ekberg had lived with them for a spell. His beloved Aunt Effie considered their house a sort of home base, and she would return home for the summers.

Sunday family dinners were a mainstay in their family. Della (his mother) would make a big family dinner the one Sunday, and then his aunt would make the next. After the meal, Gordon would play with his cousins. Though my father was an only child, he considered his cousins "the three girls" — Jean, Marilyn and Eileen — as his sisters. As the story goes, one day when my dad was young someone asked him, "Do you have brothers?...or sisters?"...and Dad said, "Yeah – three sisters!" ... Well, asked the inquiring mind ... "where do they live?" ... "At their house - across the field," said my dad.

The Ekberg family had a tradition of celebrating Christmas Eve at the farm. Being Scandanavian, lutefisk was served with all the trimmings. Then Scripture was read and songs were sung (a tradition that has continued to this day).

After the Christmas meal, Gordon would disappear as he mentioned he needed to turn a light out in the chicken coop. Shortly thereafter, Santa's sleigh bells were heard and his younger cousins would discover a load of Christmas presents that had appeared on the porch. And a little while later Gordon came in from the coop.

When he married my Mom, they settled into creating their own home. I remember my mom making huge, special meals for wildlife artists, lifelong friends, and relatives from Norway, Chicago and points across the country. There were always wonderful conversations, and I remember being fascinated as a girl listening to everything that was being shared.

Though he lived in the country, Lawndale Farm was never secluded. Over the years endless streams of people have come through from hired men, business patrons, cars and vans and bus loads of tourists and overnight guests in the bed & breakfast—and now at the lodge, and friends old – and new—stopping in to talk about the current, local hot topic or to reminisce about the old days.

At one point in his younger life he "went on the road" selling concessions for his good friend Muggs Townsend. Dad said he learned so much from this experience and enjoyed those days with good friends. Amongst the lessons we learned were ways to save money—Dad told us about a friend's practice of putting his vehicle in neutral as he came into Herman in an effort to conserve gasoline. And Dad relayed often the precise science of reeling in a customer, which included—amongst other things—implementing the correct timing (often marked by a customer passing a particular crack in a sidewalk) by simply asking "Hot dog?"

While Gordon lived at the farmhouse his whole life, his family weren't his only companions in the house. At various points there were calves in the bathtubs, love birds in the kitchen, swans in the pantry, lambs in the backroom and incubators full of chicks or ducklings in the basement ... then, to Mother's horror, in the kitchen! He loved his home.

Gordon Ekberg was a country gentleman with the ability to talk with the high and mighty, but instead would prefer to sit and visit with the widow down the road. He didn't have a lot of money, yet was rich. I don't know when it happens in this whole process, but soon – Gordon will get to touch the face of God....God will say, "Well done, good and faithful servant, well done. Enter into my kingdom. I have a special place for you in Heaven. It's over there – it's between the cattails and the bulrushes."

Those words are from Randy Larson during my dad's memorial service. My dad lived his life full and right up to the end. He finished all the chapters for his book and sent it in to the editor just five days before his passing. His book will be called *Between the Cattails and the Bulrushes*—the title he used for a column he wrote for years (maybe more than 40 … it's A LOT) for the *American Pheasant and Waterfowl Society*.

Because of my dad, I am convinced that the best way to live a life is to contribute to others, be a person of character and when you do something—give it your all. There will be two years displayed on your tombstone—make the most that you can out of that dash.

Now you may have noted that only three of his five children are listed as speaking. Don't worry about Vangie and John – they high-fived each other when they found out they didn't have to get up here to speak. However, they still wanted to share their words. Words my siblings here have shared so echo my sentiments as well. And here are their words.

Vangie:

It is no secret that phone conversations with dad were difficult. When I was in college, I was upset over breaking up with a boyfriend. I called home to unload my sadness on my mom. Dad answered the phone and said that Mom wasn't home. I was so upset and wary of a phone conversation with Dad but when I needed love and support, and a working ear, Dad came through. I cried over how upset I was and wondered out loud if I would ever find anyone. Dad shared his struggles finding "The One" and ended with how he thought he might not find someone but when he met Mom she was worth the wait.... There was a long pause and I cried, exasperated, "But I don't want to wait until I'm FORTY!!!!!"

Growing up on a family farm we spent a lot of time together. I remember riding with Dad in the feed truck to town, there were holes in the floorboard and I would watch the road pass by under my feet. Dad bought me my favorite baby doll when he was on trip as a special surprise, I remember skipping down the sidewalk holding Dad's hand as he walked tall with his cowboy hat on. We didn't have much in the way of monetary riches, but he gave us experiences and love worth far more than money can buy, I am forever grateful for that and will miss him dearly.

Dad loved us all very much, there was never any doubt. One of the ways he demonstrated his love was through making us hot homemade breakfasts every morning before school: Austrian pancakes, pancakes and bacon, scrambled eggs, French toast or Denver sandwiches. You couldn't get out the door without eating, and if you were too late and it happened to be something portable, like pancakes, he'd spread butter and sprinkle them with brown sugar and roll them up in tinfoil and send it with you, that and a hug and a kiss. We never parted without a hug and a kiss, and an "I love you."

Dad and I had a ritual of every time we returned home and pulled into the driveway, he would say, "Home Again, Home Again." And I would answer, "Jiggety Jig". Dad, I know you are at home with our Father in Heaven.

Home again, home again. Jiggety Jig.

John:
I wanted to pass on a few words about Dad. Growing up on Lawndale Farm I believed that I was one of the luckiest kids that I knew. To grow up with Dad teaching me about ducks, geese, swans and the environment was a highlight in my life. We enjoyed working together on building duck pens, cattle corrals, and a hunting shack. We also worked together having 3rd graders coming by the bus loads, taking tours and eating the famous Belgian Waffles.

When I was in the second grade he brought me up to the Red Lake Refuge where we would have our deer hunting group. This was such a big event because it meant not only did I get to go hunting with Dad, but I would get out of school for almost a whole week! I thought I was never going to see him shoot a deer, even though he said that he had shot over 45 deer in his lifetime. I finally was fortunate enough to witness this when I was a freshman in College when he shot a doe on our farm.

Also, growing up I did start to realize that he was a little older than the other dads, but I thought that was great! Especially as I got older I really liked it when me and Dad would meet someone new because nine out of ten times they would ask, "So, is this your grandson?"

I always felt lucky when my friends and I would compare what we'd eaten for breakfast. My dad's hot, homemade breakfast vs. their bowl of cold Cocoa Puffs.

Other memories that, when I think of Dad, is him always having stories, and he loved to talk to people and was interested in their lives and families. Everyone knew that you couldn't just stop in for 10 minutes, you had to at least put an hour aside. I thought we hit the lottery when the phone company went to a flat rate for long distance phone calls!!

I will miss when Dad would call me John-John, like President Kennedy called his son. He always was interested in what I was doing, and with a big smile give me a hand shake as if to say, "Hi and love you." Dad will be missed by his family, community and throughout the nation. I think he knew someone in almost every state. At one time or another he was my teacher, barber, chiropractor, counselor—he always could shed light on a dark situation. He also was my friend, my hero—and what makes me the proudest is when someone would say "Ekberg? Is Gordon Ekberg your dad?" I would have this great joy inside of me and privilege to say "Yes, he is!"

Dad, I will miss you so much and love you for all eternity.

Kris Ann:
For those of you who don't know me, I am Kris Ann Erickson, the eldest of the Ekberg kids. I live in Menomonie, Wisconsin, with my husband Dale and our four boys, Jake, Tobey, Xander and Levi.

Thank you all so much for coming today to celebrate and

remember Dad's very full and very well-lived life. I've no doubt that he was many things to many people (Odd Fellow, Environmentalist, Author, Farmer, Entrepreneur, Steward of the Land, Country Vet, Hunter, Trapper, and more). He accomplished much, was involved in much, and led the way in much.

To me, of course, he was just "Dad" ... but even this title encompasses so much more than the word itself implies. He created for us a legacy of family, fun, faith and stewardship.

Dad was a REALLY FUN dad. He taught us that it was okay ... and even best ... for adults to be playful. Some of my earliest memories of Dad are of him crawling around the ground on all fours while I sat on his back with my legs wrapped tight around his middle and my hands clinging eagerly to the back of his flannel work shirt. These were "bear rides". Now, I am not really sure that most bears are "rideable" but in Dad's opinion, if you could ride a bear, it would run around the house really fast, and then would rear up or buck on occasion ... a lot like a horse. Except it wouldn't "whinny", it would "rawr".

He taught us outdoor games like *Fox and Goose* in the winter, and *Kick the Can* in the summer.

Dad was always a really good sport. He would come in the house at the hottest part of the day to take a little siesta on the living room floor. When Amy and I were small, he would let us put our plastic barrettes and pink foam rollers in his hair while he rested there.

Storytelling was a huge part of the fabric of family. While Mom regularly read to us, Dad chose to weave together stories for us from his experiences. I was always amazed at his creativity. The subjects of his stories were usually woodland creatures ... like Chippy the Chipmunk ... or Skunky the Skunk ... or Squirrely the Squirrel ... and he always incorporated lots of drama, and added some moral (generally the moral was that you ought to listen to your parents.)

Dad was a natural born teacher. Not only were his stories an opportunity for him to teach us a thing or two, but everything and anything that crossed our path was a teaching opportunity. If a skink crossed our path, he'd pick it up and teach us about its tail (which it drops to escape predators). Time to butcher something? He invited us to watch and learn all about the skeletal structure, the circulatory system, the respiratory system, etc. We have had snapping turtle hearts beating in the fridge for weeks, preserved in salt water. We have had ducklings in our sink to revive them. He taught us the names and origins of all the ducks, geese and swan species he collected, and it is still a point of pride to me that I possess this unique knowledge.

One of my favorite memories as a mom has been bringing my boys to the farm, and watching Dad teach them. Traditionally, every farm visit includes a truck tour of the back 80 acres, most of which is prairie and marsh. The kids pile into the truck, some in the cab, some in the bed, and we bounce along the rutted dirt road, making frequent stops so that Grandpa can teach. He sees a lesson in everything ... the plums, the wild crab apples, the goldenrod laden with larvae, the bird in the air, the duck in the pond, the snake in the grass.

Besides having fun ... and working hard ... Dad's faith was so important to him. Before he had his own children, Dad taught other people's children about the gift of salvation through Sunday School. Dad's favorite verse was John 3:16, "*For God so loved the world that He gave His only begotten son that whosoever believeth in Him will not perish but have everlasting life.*"

Just yesterday, we discovered a treasure that Dad left behind for us. It was a letter that he began on December 31, 1995, and completed on July 15, 1997. In it, he speaks passionately about how important his relationship with God has been. He also squeezes in a "little more moral advice" and speaks of his love for the family farm and his passion for the land and our responsibility to steward it well. I'd like to share that with you this morning.

> *December 31, 1995 - July 15,1997*
> *It's about 4 o'clock and I thought that I had better write out a few notes about a funeral for myself. I would like the text of the funeral sermon to be on John 3:16. It may seem simple, but I like it and put my trust in Him. Gay,*

you have made my life complete. You didn't get to Paris nor fly a plane (during my lifetime) (but she did go to Paris!) but we did have fun! I have enjoyed the family life that we have had. The kids have been great. I'm proud of each one. I had always thought that I would like to leave a personal letter to each one of you but will put my thoughts in this short letter to all of you. I do hope that all of you will hang on with a fierce tenacity to a trust in Jesus Christ. I don't mean polishing a halo nor feeling that you have "lost it" if you didn't get to church on Sunday. I do mean trusting God and walking with Him each day. I didn't read Scripture every day of my life, but I did talk (pray) to Him most every day. These last few years, many times a day ... before most every decision, phone call or what I perceived might be a difficult encounter. He was there! So, the best advice that I can give is "Don't ever lose your contact with God (In Jesus Name) if you do, GET IT BACK! Don't ever think that I, Gordon Ekberg, merited salvation. I didn't, I was loaded with frailties. I was weighed on the scales of justice and found wanting, to me it was my acceptance of Jesus Christ as my personal savior that tipped the scales for my salvation.

Just a little moral advice ... Don't' smoke, if I had I would have been dead much sooner. Flee drugs like the plague... and keep in mind that the most subtle and damaging of all drugs is alcohol. You don't' show maturity drinking beer and having cocktails ... you just lower your stature and dull your mind. Marry believers and give them respect and love. Help your mother whenever she needs help (and even if she doesn't need help, surprise her with some kindly deed of love and kindness) and care for her in her old age.

Our home farm (235 acres) is to me, not a commodity to be bought and sold, I look at it as the Scriptures say we should … as a sacred trust. I hope that the boys, if they choose, or the girls, if they choose, will be able to work together and have a happy and productive life. This keeping the farm is not a deathbed mandate, but it is certainly a sincere wish to keep the farm in the family. I love you all very much! Thanks for being such a wonderful wife and family.

I'd like to close with a poem. Dad LOVED poems, and had many of them memorized. He sure enjoyed reciting them, too … and any time he had a captive audience, he couldn't resist sharing one.

I'll close with one of his favorites, *The Touch of the Master's Hand* by Myra Brooks Welch. For Dad, who placed his life in the Master's Hand, and the result has been rich and beautiful and full.

The Touch of the Master's Hand

'Twas battered and scarred, and the auctioneer
  Thought it scarcely worth his while
To waste much time on the old violin,
  But held it up with a smile.
"What am I bidden, good folks," he cried,
  "Who'll start the bidding for me?"
"A dollar, a dollar. Then two! Only two?
  Two dollars, and who'll make it three?"

"Three dollars, once; three dollars, twice;
  Going for three…" But no,
From the room, far back, a grey-haired man
  Came forward and picked up the bow;
Then wiping the dust from the old violin,
  And tightening the loosened strings,

He played a melody pure and sweet,
  As a caroling angel sings.
The music ceased, and the auctioneer,
  With a voice that was quiet and low,
Said: "What am I bid for the old violin?"
  And he held it up with the bow.
"A thousand dollars, and who'll make it two?
  Two thousand! And who'll make it three?
Three thousand, once; three thousand, twice,
  And going and gone," said he.

The people cheered, but some of them cried,
  "We do not quite understand.
What changed its worth?" Swift came the reply:
  "The touch of the Master's hand."
And many a man with life out of tune,
  And battered and scarred with sin,
Is auctioned cheap to the thoughtless crowd
  Much like the old violin.

A "mess of pottage," a glass of wine,
  A game — and he travels on.
He is "going" once, and "going" twice,
  He's "going" and almost "gone."
But the Master comes, and the foolish crowd
  Never can quite understand
The worth of a soul and the change that is wrought
  By the touch of the Master's hand.

Awards

Some of Gordon Ekberg's Awards
and Accomplishments
(Compiled Postumously)

Independent Order of Odd Fellows (IOOF):

Member of IOOF Harmony Lodge, Herman, MN, since January 1948

Joined Encampment in 1950

Signed up over 157 new IOOF members

Served in positions at local, state, and national and international levels

Received Meritorious Service Award

Received medals and pins for years of membership

Received awards from various visiting dignitaries at annual Grand Lodge
gatherings in Minnesota

Served 3 terms District Deputy Grand Patriarch

1959 — Grand Patriarch of the Grand Encampment of Minnesota

Chartered a new encampment

Organized Encampment Royal Purple Entertainers

Served on Grand Encampment Youth Committee for 9 years

Chartered Theta Rho Girls Club in Herman

Served on Sovereign Grand Lodge committees

Had perfect attendance for the first 23 consecutive years

Served as Grand Master of Minnesota in 1962-1963
  (attended about 160 meetings around the state)
  (Named Outstanding Grand Master of North American continent)

Grand Representative for 8 years

International Officer 1970

Representative of Minnesota to International Convention (6 years)

Major (R) Canton Caledonia #18: 1960 Declaration of Chivalry

Sovereign Grand Lodge Patriarch's Militant Award to
Captain Gordon F. Ekberg

Sovereign Grand Lodge Chairman of Film Committee

Sovereign Grand Lodge – 8 years on Legislative Committee

Member of Rebekah Lodge for over 50 years

Sovereign Grand Messenger for Donald R. Smith of California

Presided over 400 Odd Fellow funeral rites

1958 — Started annual Smelt Fry at the Odd Fellows Lodge, Herman

1979 — Annual IOOF Hall of Fame award at Herman, given for unselfish
leadership in church, lodge, community, and conservation.

Published a monthly column "Along this Rugged Path"

Church:

Confirmed at Bethel Lutheran Church

Married at United Methodist Church and became a member

In later years, Gordon and Gay joined the Bethlehem West Elbow Lake
Lutheran Church in Elbow Lake

Lay leader

Lay speaker for pulpit supply for area churches

Board member

Sunday School teacher for High School

Local Government and Community Positions:

Active in DFL, Precinct Chairman

Chairman of Senator Wayne Olhoft Volunteer Committee

Volunteer Committee for Representative Carl Iverson

Macsville Township Clerk

Ran for DFL endorsement for Congress in 1977 for the position vacated by Bob Berglund, who had been appointed Secretary of Agriculture

First President of County Association of Township Officers

Grant County Red Cross

Lakeside Cemetery Association, Director (15 years)

County Farmers Home Administration, President

Herman Investment Club, President, Secretary

Memberships:

Farmers Union

National Farmers Organization (county president, secretary, public relations, author of monthly column, extensive speaking engagements)

American Angus Association

American Simmental Association

Columbia Sheep Breeders Association of America

Honorary member of Future Farmers of America, Herman chapter

Hobbies:

Raising wild waterfowl

Camping

Hunting

Fishing

Trapping

Farming:

3rd generation farmer at Lawndale Farm (Ekberg the 2nd oldest name in the Herman area since 1875, next to Niemackl family in 1872)

2002 Century Farm Award from Grant County Farm Bureau

Farmed 560 acres at one time (wheat, barley, beans and corn)

Raised Spotted Poland China hogs

Developed herds of registered Holstein dairy cattle, registered Angus beef cattle and Simmental beef cattle

Raised flocks of registered Columbia and Suffolk sheep

Had several hives of bees, also appreciated landscaping and flowers

One of 168 farm families to be recognized by *Successful Farming* magazine's "Farming in the Flyways" program, which promotes farming coexisting with wildlife

Environment:

Dedicated to good stewardship of the land and natural resources, ardent admirer of Aldo Leopold and his work

Member of several national and international waterfowl groups Wrote "Between the Cattails and the Bulrushes" for *APWS Magazine*, published by the American Pheasant and Waterfowl Association

1980 — Certificate of Merit from the Fergus Falls Area Save and Restore the Wetlands, recognizing his contributions to the preservation of wetlands, signed by DNR, U.S. Fish & Wildlife Service, U.S. Soil Conservation Service

1986 Award Plaque "*In grateful appreciation for your contributions to Minnesota Pheasant and Waterfowl Society*"

2003 — American Pheasant and Waterfowl Society Outstanding Service Award for his column "Between the Cattails and the Bulrushes"

Built breeding pen for canvasback ducks, modeled after one he toured at Delta Waterfowl Research Station in Canada

Lawndale Environmental Foundation, Inc., received *1996 Outstanding Organization Award* by Wesmin RC and D Council (the center that evolved from Gordon's educational waterfowl display and involvement of waterfowl artists)

Emperor Geese on Lawndale Farm were used as models for Dan Smith's painting, winning First of State for Alaska duck stamp contest

Northwest Sportsmen's Regional Award

Fergus Falls Fish and Game Club Award

Eyton Tree Ducks on Lawndale Farm were also models for Dan Smith's painting First of Nation duck stamp for Australia

1986 Conservationist of the Year/Pioneer award from the Minnesota Waterfowl Association, given for work to help waterfowl prosper

July 1988 — Set up display of live Lesser Snow Geese for first issue of a waterfowl stamp by Dan Smith at the Eden Prairie Post Office, covered by national television

Set up display of live waterfowl for an artist print release by Jim Hautman at the Mall of America

April 1991 — Earth Day celebration tours of the prairie on two hayracks, educational event hosted at Lawndale Farm, sponsored by the LEF. Ken and Evelyn Morrell with son Hugh Matheisen served food out of their tent: biscuits/gravy, strawberry shortcake and funnel cakes.

Newspaper and Magazine Coverage/Recognition:

Herman Review

Herman-Hoffman Tribune

Grant County Herald

Wheaton Gazette

Morris Sun Tribune

Echo Press (Alexandria)

Fergus Falls Daily Journal

Fargo Forum

Minneapolis Star Tribune (Ron Schara Sunday edition feature story)

Kadiak Times (Alaska – first trip)

Associated Press (carried nationwide)

APWS Magazine

Farm and Ranch Living (nationwide)

Minnesota Waterfowler

Successful Farming and the NFO magazine

Television Coverage/Interviews:

Channel 7 (Alexandria)

WCCO "On the Road Again with Jason Davis"

Channel 11 "Mel Stone Report"
Channel 10 "Venture North"
Cable (White Bear Lake) Australian Duck Stamp
Channel 11 "Insight" with Doug Hamilton
WCCO Ron Schara

Other Exposure/Recognition to Lawndale Farm:

Lawndale Farm plays host to 4,000 to 5,000 visitors per year, including students of all ages from area schools, Headstart through grade 12, college students and instructors (the most recent being from University of Minnesota and North Dakota State University), as well as artists and environmental researchers from throughout the United States and Canada.

1988 — Letter of Congratulation from Minnesota Governor Rudy Perpich, commending Lawndale Farm on their B & B.

Gordon was mentor twice for students from University of Minnesota-Crookson who worked/learned at Lawndale Farm and earned credits in the waterfowl management department. After the three month internship, Gordon also provided a written test.

Sign near restored marsh: Improving Waterfowl Habitat: A cooperative effort involving Ducks Unlimited, U.S. Fish and Wildlife Service and Gordon Ekberg.

Took part in a campaign ad for US WEST Communications, featured in newspapers and radio ads featuring Gordon as part of the script (recorded at the Foshay tower), supporting telemedicine network.

Dale Carnegie graduate
Award from Citizens Bank, Morris, Minnesota
Numerous other community awards

(This list of awards was compiled posthumously from newspaper clippings, wall plaques/certificates, and Gordon's IOOF notations.)

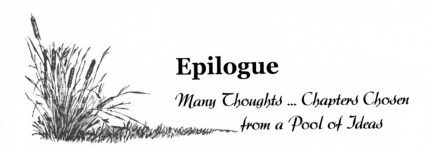

Epilogue
Many Thoughts ... Chapters Chosen
from a Pool of Ideas

When sorting and reviewing Gordon's many materials, pages listing ideas for potential chapters were discovered after Gordon passed. The titles and thoughts suggest further events of his time. A single page with the heading "Possible Chapters" was the beginning of his eliminating and condensing these pages into a list of the chapter titles. Hopefully, this is not an invasion of privacy, but another glance into the times of his life. Some of these titles and possible content included:

Corn Picking

Bee Swarming

Aunt Annie's Visit from Canada

Cutting Corn and Shocking: Building Sawhorses for Shocking

Dad Breaking Babe and Other Horses on Frank Marth's Slough

Babe Walked on Hind Legs 2/3rds of Time

Neighbor Shorthorn White Bull Fighting

Cleaning the Barn with Both Manure Carrier and Wheelbarrow

Butchering a Beef and 2 or 3 Hogs in a Day: Making Blood Sausage

Grandpa Ekberg Moved Here in 1938 (Grandma Ekberg died May 1938.)

Gordon further listed "ideas" to include in the book:

* *I have up to nine hives of bees as a 12 year old.*
* *I do a lot of bee removal where bees are unwanted in houses.*
  Bee removal from Les Asmus- 17 stings.
* *I do Blueberries and learn a new method of fertilizer*
* *We have a lot of berries and plums*
* *Verlyn Marth and Prairies*
* *My first big lecture-Luther League* (on bees)
* *My first framing job* (Gordon initially framed for the gallery)
* *Runaway horse*
* *Family Thanksgiving and Christmas* (Christmas Eve was held at home with relatives coming here)
* *Lost in the Woods*
* *Lunch on the lawn, cinnamon rolls and coffee at 3:30*
* *Reuss, our friends and neighbors, brought melons to share at school*
* *Shelling Corn, Pete Ennen and Art Drexler*
* *Brood sows*
* *Milton Lueneberg:* (When dividing crows, Milt shot Gordon in the seat with a BB gun, so he rolled down the roof to give Milt a scare.)
* *Plastering hen house*
* *Showing at the fair* (sheep for example)
* *Laying hens:* Buff orpington, Rhode Island Reds, New Hampshire Red, Anacona, White Giants and White Rock, Leghorns
* *Aunt Effie's clothes went out the roof of the house* (a huge wind caused a suction that pulled her clothes from the closet up though the adjacent attic stairway and through an opening in the attic)
* *How did sows get little pigs? (Found in straw)*
* *I couldn't carry a tune, could I?* (Gordon had been told all his life he couldn't sing, but when Gay took voice lessons from Carlin Berg,

Elbow Lake, Gordon also took individual voice lessons. Carlin praised Gordon for his wide range of voice and he discovered he could sing!)

* *Ice cream making, Butter churning, Grinding coffee, Hatching eggs*

* *Turkey money bought piano for Mom and Auntie. Both could play by ear.*

* *Grandpa Gord could play accordion and harmonica by ear, Grandma Gord played the zither.*

* *Preparing for winter*

* *I. R. Ekberg, The cousins*

* *Digging silo pit*

* *Ice house*

* *Cooking in summer*

* *Prairie Chickens booming*

* *Harry's Haberdashery*

* *Circus in Fergus*

* *Lynx in neighborhood* (At Christmas time as a youth, Gordon was taking packages out to the car, when he came back in the house quite alarmed because of the awful sound he heard out there. His dad didn't see what could be so bad so he went out and also returned quite alarmed. The sound of the lynx was just blood curdling.)

* *Got my mouth washed out with soap*

* *Coon hunting with Patsy* (his dog)

* *Moving building from George Kreidler farm*

* *Tom cat killing kittens*

* *Sleigh and sauerkraut*

* *Julebukking*

* *Jean Rae and I sitting on Grandma Ekberg's lap as a special treat while she sliced apples saying…* (wonder what she said!)

* *Grandpa and Grandma get a Norge electric refrigerator*

* *We rent Reuss' portion of land at Louie's request. I have an arrangement with Louie for sheep to glean fields, we also feed cattle*

over there! Louie and I have a fish house on Upper Pomme de Terre—our first fish house was our Smoke House, which we hauled on our truck. It is now our well house. Louie takes me fishing many times in the summer. We always had family meals at each other's homes in the winter.

* *Scrapbook Tour – Gordon's mother-in-law did a fabulous job with a scissors* (She had saved all the newspaper articles.)

* *Hummingbirds on Apple Trees*

* *Del Holdgrafer and Ernie Strubbe*

* *The REA came through, Montgomery Ward does wrong.* (REA came in 1935; in 1944 President of U.S. chastised Montgomery Ward business for not being in war effort)

* *Morning Lunch at 9*

* *Fanning Mill*

* *Grasshoppers*

* *Haying*

* *Lilacs in bloom*

* *Big 2 Cycling Case with roof ran threshing machine*

* *Dad comes home with new radio from selling cattle at South St. Paul*

* *Grandpa Gord goes sunfishing and teaches me how*

* *Harry Day of Morris hired to open ditch for drainage*

* *Uncle Tom's Duck Pond*

* *I was happy for the years we held meetings in our home* (youth/adult Christian meetings in the 1970s)

Accolades

Carole Butcher, Wordsmith, formerly of Fergus Falls:

"Gordon writes in a unique folksy style. He spins tales that are absolutely charming. His stories embody the feel of simpler times. They are both entertaining and uplifting. This work weaves together nostalgia and a remembrance of things past. He captures a sense of place and time. The characters are sharply drawn and imminently memorable."

Larry Batson, Reporter for Minneapolis Star and Tribune, on Gordon's induction into Herman's 5th annual "Hall of Fame":

"... But you don't get into the hall of fame by making money, leaving town, becoming famous, dying romantically or in any of the other usual ways. You have to stick around, carry more than your share of the community load and earn the respect and friendship of your neighbors. Then the communities of Herman and Norcross and Harmony Lodge No. 230 IOOF, will consider your nomination. Ekberg can point to an astounding list of activities—civic, church, and political, as a youth worker, agricultural activist and lodge officer. Master of Ceremonies Owen Heiberg said, 'Gordy will do anything for anyone at any time.'"

Gordon inspired a youth by sharing:

"What you say won't be remembered when you are gone, but the things you do will be."

Rich and Deanne Kennedy, educators from Herman, MN:

"I still remember Gordon's talk about the importance of cattails. He was a true teacher."

Wayne Olhoft, former Minnesota State Senator:

"He has that delightful combination of humility, story-telling ability, wisdom, and extensive life experiences which make a most delightful host and teacher ... He is a fountain of wisdom, a pillar of strength and a giant in heart. His honesty and integrity are above reproach. I have repeatedly seen him forego personal and emotional gain to preserve principle and harmony."

Larry Carlson, Past Minnesota Grand Master of IOOF:

"His faith in his God is unshakable as I believe, is the foundation for his desire to bring out and preserve the best in all mankind. Being a man of limited formal education, Gordon has elevated himself to an educational level equal to almost any man through personal effort and self-determination ... ability to make friends quickly with any person. His ability to use the English language is one of his greatest assets. Gordon and his wife Gay are raising a fine family in an atmosphere of love, hard work and faith. I have great respect for his wisdom, vision, and ability..."

Donald R. Smith, Past Sovereign Grand Master of IOOF:

"I highly recommend and commend Gordon for his many accomplishments, his vision, and enthusiasm, with the assurance that whatever he undertakes he will give his very best to make it successful."

Daniel S. Smith, nationally-known wildlife artist:

"I've never known anyone so generous, honest and hard working as Gordon. Lawndale Farm is the best game farm I've visited in the nation and Gordon Ekberg is one of the few owners generous enough to share his facility with the public."

Pastor Earl A. Almquist:

"Gordon Ekberg is a man on whom I feel I can rely. His faith and his intelligence is outstanding. And even when he is not holding an office, people in the church and the community look to him for leadership. It is a privilege to serve in the same church as him."

Van D. Gooch, former Biology professor at U of M, Morris, MN:

"Furthermore, he is enthusiastic in sharing his knowledge and extremely active in doing whatever he can to propagate knowledge."

Jerry Bryson, former banker at Herman, MN:

"He has the knack for taking something routine and making it exciting whether it is in daily activities or in public speaking. Gordon has been active in numerous civic and political groups. He is respected by them and often used as a consulting 'sounding board.' He also has the knack for taking technical material and bringing it down to a common language that can be understood by anyone, including children."

Pastor Wes and Mary Moir:

"The ride out to the prairie was awesome ... and your wonderful 'Lawndale' gave us the feeling of a very peaceful and restorative place in this tumultuous world!"